Christy's book is an easy-to-read semi-biographical reflection on the ups and down of life. She has shared her experiences honestly, with reflections on scripture, and in way that most readers will identify with.
This is a reflective and compassionate book that readers will surely be encouraged by.

—Matt Jacoby, lead band member, Sons of Korah

Sometimes you need a friend who can tell a story from her own life that makes you realize you're not the only one who's ever had a moment just like that. You might call it icing on the cake when that same friend can take those moments and help you see the Lord at work in them. Christy Cabe is that friend, and *If Only It Were a Piece of Cake* is the gift she offers you. She shares the sweet and sticky stories of her life and generously serves up the life lessons God taught her in the process. Pull up a chair and sink your teeth into the delicious gift she offers in this book!

—Bekah Shaffer, speaker and author of *His Advent: Still His Greatest Gift* and *Be Still: Learning to Know He is God.*

I teared up. I laughed out loud. I thought deeply and retrospectively. Christy transparently shares the triumphs and the tragedies in her life in order to draw us closer to Christ.

—Dr. Mitch Kruse, host of the television program, *The Restoration Road with Mitch Kruse* and author of *Restoration Road* and *Street Smarts from Proverbs.*

Like a long conversation with a good friend, Christy welcomes you into her story and speaks directly to your story. Woven with transparency, grace, hope and humor, her story is sometimes hard and heartbreaking but always pushing you toward Jesus who give us abundant life.

—Heather Gonzales
Vice President & COO, National Association of Evangelicals

Christy had me laughing at times and just sitting in silent agreement at others. So relatable and validating. It is rare to read anything that makes my heart connect and smile at the same time. Christy proves that JOY is not a result of the absence of trials, but a gift of wisdom and the reality that God is in the middle of it all. What a joy and gift to the soul!

—Kenn Kington, Comedian, Speaker, Author, All round nice guy!

Relevant, relatable, honest, and fun. Christy Cabe has a beautiful way of writing that connects to the heart! Christy connects God's timeless truth to everyday happenings - the good the bad and the ugly. If you ever wonder if you are alone, Christy writes in a very honest way that lets you know that someone gets it. She gives good biblical advice on how to navigate the parts of life that aren't such a piece of cake! Her life journey has given her good wisdom, and her love and faith in Christ are deeply at the center of it all. We highly recommend this encouraging and uplifting book.

—Angela and Mark Vincenti, Mark and Angela have served together in ministry for nearly two decades. Mark is the author of the book, *Pursuing the Third Option: Following Jesus in a Polarized World.*

Christy is a brilliant storyteller and even more importantly she combines this with profound theological clarity. Her elegant writing move the heart and challenges the will but does so through stimulating the mind with clear and accurate biblical clarity and insight. What a combination, what a great read!

—Graham Daniels, Associate Preacher, St. Andrew the Great, and General Director of Christians in Sport, Cambridge, UK

If Only It Were a
Piece of Cake

Christy Cabe

To Kelly Rich - This book is largely about living. My desire is to share hope with those who are facing difficult moments, and to encourage them to live and move forward in spite of the struggle.

As I've watched you battle cancer for the past sixteen years, you have modeled this to me, and have taught me more about living through pain than anyone I've ever known.

The humility you and Marc possess, and your desire to honor God above all else, has left an impact on many lives. Not the least of which is mine. I am honored to call you a friend, and hope I can help encourage and teach what you have taught me.

I love you, friend.

how we'll slice it

foreword

When my wife, Christy, asked me to write this foreword, I said, "That is a little forward of you to ask such a thing!"

Christy and I have spent nearly two decades together. First as friends, then dating, and now over sixteen years of marriage. There have been many laughs and some tears. Sometimes my attempts at humor have been so bad it's nearly brought her to tears (see above). We've seen dreams turn into reality and some not come to fruition. We've experienced the joys that come with parenting three great kids and we've experienced the heartache of sickness and loss.

In Christy's first book, *Brownie Crumbs and Other Life Morsels,* she shares some of the more public highs and lows of her life: the death of her mother when Christy was a child, our dating and marriage, and our cancer journey with our son.

In this book, Christy opens the window to some of our more private experiences and all of the accompanying emotions—anger, disappointment, contentment, and joy. At the same time, she shares some of the things she has learned about herself, me as her husband, and most importantly, our amazing God.

Throughout *If Only It Were a Piece of Cake* you will get a glimpse into some personal discussions—and yes, some disagreements—Christy and I have had through the years. We've had to have some difficult conversations and our competitive natures sometimes come out. (She says I can be quietly stubborn, but I'll never admit to it!)

Please know that everything Christy has shared is written with my blessing and is an accurate account. We share it to encourage you and to remind you that sometimes life isn't a "piece of cake," but it's still worth living.

Christy is the love of my life, one of the wisest people I know, a great wife, mom, and friend. I have had the blessing of gleaning from her thoughts for nearly twenty years. It's my hope this book will bless you like she has blessed me.

-Kraig Cabe

introduction

on life and cake

My oven is cold. The cake stand is empty.

I have a cake mix in the pantry, but it can't be eaten straight from the box. The powder requires oil, eggs, and some elbow grease.

Meanwhile, at my door, Opportunity is knocking. Life is asking me to let it in fully. But I'm hesitant to do so. The excuse of no cake to serve is disguising the bigger reason; engaging with Life requires effort and often leads to difficulties. Opportunity brings baggage: worry, anxiety, change, guilt, loss, anger, discontentment, insecurity, and more. I'm not sure how there's room for socks and underwear.

Sometimes it's easier to ignore the knocking. To avoid the effort. To disengage from living.

Life. If only it were a piece of cake! But it's not. Even the good things can bring difficulties in tow.

Just because life is difficult to deal with doesn't mean we shouldn't live it. And live it in the midst of the difficult moments.

I've shared on my blog, *Ten Blue Eyes*, over the years, about some struggles in which I seem to specialize. Not that I want to specialize in them. I'd rather conquer them. But I haven't yet, and so instead, I write about them.

As I wrote this book, and organized each chapter to deal with a difficult life topic, I decided to include some of my previously posted blog essays with each respective issue. I figured I might as well share my original words and reflections from that season or moment. These blog essays almost serve as a journal entry of sorts, incorporated into the book where they best apply.

I wish I could also serve up the answers to all of life's problems, but I don't have them. I wouldn't even begin to pretend to!

So, I offer you all I can: some honesty, hope, and companionship amidst the journey.

At the end of each chapter, you'll find a "Slice of Hope." It's a short thought that may offer help for that difficult topic. And guess what? You can have it, and eat it too! I'm nice like that.

Finally, I provide some discussion and application questions in the back of the book in "Cakewalk." Maybe they can help you, or your small group, take the next steps to apply the ideas of hope to your daily stride.

Pour a glass of milk, and let's get started!

one

worry and anxiety

I stood frozen and unblinking. I held my breath, trying to listen. Trying to prepare for the moment of impact. I was waiting for the other shoe to drop.

And it did.

It was a size-five boys black dress shoe, to be exact, hitting the ceramic tile on the lower floor of our home.

I had already heard what I surmised to be the first shoe dropping. Thhuuuuumpp!!

In that super-speed mom-brain mode that can think faster than the Road Runner can get away from Wile E. Coyote, I knew what had happened. It was a Sunday morning, and our then seven-year-old son was getting dressed for church. I knew I had laid out his black dress shoes. I also knew that since recently moving into a home with a second-story landing, that our son discovered a newfound interest in gravity. I thought I had made it clear that no "hard objects" were to be dropped below, but with seven-year-old boys I should have been a bit more specific.

So I waited. I waited for the other shoe to drop. It thumped as loudly as the first, and the sound reverberated off the walls and tile floor. I twisted shut the lid to my mascara and placed it back in the drawer. Then I found Karson in the hallway. We reviewed the "landing rule." Dropping hard objects is not good for the walls, floor, objects being dropped, or little sisters who happen to be standing below. Lesson learned, it appeared, and so we moved on with our Sunday morning.

But, as I was blowing my hair dry, I thought about it some more. I had literally just waited for the other shoe to drop. I figuratively do it so often that it was interesting to actually experience it for real!

I sometimes use the phrase "waiting for the other shoe to drop" when trying to explain how I feel about fear. I struggle with fearing what big, hard trial will happen next in my life.

I've had some whoppers of a "shoe drop" in my past. My mother's sudden death when I was in fifth grade. A cancer diagnosis for our two-year-old son. Miscarriages. These things all contribute to my struggle with fear.

Because I know that shoes do fall, when things are going well, I sometimes find myself waiting for the next one to smack the floor. Before I know it, I'm frozen, unblinking, and holding my breath. Instead of enjoying life and living in the moment, I'm listening. I'm waiting for that figurative other shoe. It can be torturous.

The accessibility I have to the Internet worsens this for me. Maybe this is true for other shoe-waiters as well. I find myself scrolling through Facebook, or reading the news headlines, and suddenly fear seizes me. It's like hypochondria, only broader to encompass things beyond the health-related. Fearing that all of the awful headlines I read or hear about are going to happen to me. A school shooting at my child's school, a giant sinkhole suddenly opening in my front yard and swallowing up someone I love, a deadly nuclear attack in my neighborhood, an outbreak the CDC is warning about sweeping through my city, a deranged and deadly alligator on my back patio (I live in Indiana). I imagine it all in detail.

Twitter also poses a problem for me in the sense that it's so blunt and time specific. I follow my local news stations on Twitter, and they report traffic accidents in 280 characters or less. They frankly state that there has been a crash on a specific road and sometimes they throw in the two words, "with injuries." I am affected and afflicted by these tweets. I cannot simply scroll past them without caring. I worry that someone I know was involved in the crash. I worry for those who were injured. My worrisome thoughts exceed 280 characters, without a cut off.

Speaking of being cut off, Kraig told me one evening that he was going outside to fix the riding lawn mower and to install a new belt on the mower deck. My immediate response was, "Please don't cut your arms off." I was serious. He was going to be working near a sharp blade. Granted, the chances of him actually cutting his arms off, especially both arms, seems pretty drastic, but I needed to issue this warning anyway. As with most every time I make such a ridiculous statement of concern, Kraig responded with, "Oh, thanks. I was planning to cut my arms off, but now I won't." Then he rolls his eyes, winks, and walks away. I'm glad I'm getting through to him.

I hate, I repeat, hate, living in this state of mind. Worry and anxiety are lies, and they steal from my peace and joy. But, knowing this doesn't change the fact that I deal with their ugliness on a regular basis. That's why it's a struggle.

I know for a fact that every awful thing I hear about could not possibly all happen to me. If my neighborhood is taken out by a nuclear attack, then the alligator is probably toast too. But, I have such a vivid imagination, it only takes a little fuel to ignite a blazing fire of worry and anxiety.

It's unhealthy and exhausting. Admitting that I deal with this on a regular basis is also embarrassing. But, admitting a struggle is also one of the first steps toward healing. I'm all for healing. I want to beat this. I am a competitive woman. (More on that later.)

I also know I'm not alone in this struggle. At least a few of my friends have admitted to me they live in a similar battle with worry and anxiety. Recently, one of my friends was telling me about a concern she and her husband had over a potential health issue with one of their children. She had imagined some possible worst-case scenarios. So, when this child yelled for her from the bathroom, "Mom! I need you!" she ran in there afraid. Turns out the child just needed more shampoo in the shower.

When she told me this story, I just wanted to hug her. Because *I get it*. First of all, when will our children learn to take inventory of the shampoo situation before getting into the shower? Second, I've run that crazy fear-filled route myself many times. It doesn't matter if it's toward the bathroom, the basement, or the backyard; it's scary every time.

I know we're not the only two people on Earth who have experienced this awful anticipation brought to us by fear, worry, and anxiety, and fueled by an active imagination.

The incident that most clearly proved a current of fear runs just under the surface happened outside on a beautiful spring day. You see, it doesn't even have to be a dark and stormy night to make my fears and worries present themselves. Bright and calm evenings work as well.

Kraig and I, and the kids, signed up to participate in a local 5K race to support some friends. We had participated in previous years, and we knew the course fairly well. It's close to our home. Kraig, Karly, and Karson like to run most of the course. Kenzie and I walk.

We decided one evening to drive to our local high school, where the course began, park our van there, and then run, or walk, the roughly three-mile loop back to the van. The course is basically a large square.

For the first three sides of the square, Kenzie and I walked, but could see the other three running ahead of us, though they moved further away with each turn of a corner. We had planned that the three of them would run back to the van and Kenzie and I would continue straight toward our own neighborhood. This made sense. By the time we walked the entire course, they would have to wait for us awhile, so we might as well walk home and meet them there.

Kenzie and I walked hand-in-hand down the path beside the road. We passed many others out jogging or walking in the lovely evening atmosphere. I was trying hard to savor the time with my youngest child and to feel her sweet, soft, warm hand in mine.

We walked past our local fire station. As we did, an alarm sounded and over the outside speaker system, a woman's voice could be heard robotically reading an emergency bulletin.

"We have a twelve-year-old who has been struck by a vehicle. Please respond."

I stopped dead in my tracks.

My son, Karson, was twelve years old. He was running at that very moment, crossing intersections where vehicles very well could have hit him.

My heart was beating out of my chest. I couldn't breathe.

I stood with Kenzie by my side and dialed Kraig's number on my cell phone.

So many horrible images played in my mind. In only a matter of seconds, an entire reel of footage had been cast, directed, filmed, and played in my mind's eye. The content was graphic and disturbing.

"Hello?" Kraig answered.

"Are you guys alright?" I said breathlessly.

"Yeah, why?"

The tears began. I started to sob.

"Christy? What's going on?"

I couldn't stop crying.

I finally told Kraig about the emergency call at the fire station. That I feared it was Karson.

"That's awful, but it wasn't Karson. We're fine. We're back in the van and heading your way now." Kraig assured me.

We hung up and I slowly began to walk. I looked down at Kenzie and she was crying too.

"I thought it was Karson!" she wailed in her little seven-year-old voice.

"Me too, baby. Me too."

We walked slowly, hand-in-hand again. Both crying.

Then the thought hit me that even though it wasn't my son, a car had hit someone's son, and I felt terrible for them. I began to pray silently for whoever it was. God knew the details.

Our van passed us and Kraig pulled into the road ahead and parked along the curb. Kenzie ran up and hopped in.

I was still a mess. I hadn't calmed down yet and I was thankful I was wearing sunglasses to hide my wet eyes. I told Kraig I needed to walk the rest of the way home by myself to regain my composure. He drove away with the kids and gave me some space.

I cried for several more minutes.

The emotions and fears that hide dormant, but alive, just under the surface of my soul awake easily—and not to a groggy and slow-moving state, but to an active and laser-focused condition able to wreak havoc on my mind and heart.

It's as if I'm a human version of Chicken Little, who waited for the sky to fall, only I'm waiting for a shoe. My feathers get ruffled so very easily as I anticipate the impact.

At seven years, Karson dropped his shoes over the railing of the landing and made an impact on my thinking. It was a visual representation of how I live.

When Karson was twelve, the fear that he had been struck by a car sent me into a crying tizzy. Once again, I realized that I was waiting for a shoe to drop. Only now, Karson wore a size twelve. Bigger shoes are falling, folks. These things leave a mark.

Time progresses, but the passage of time doesn't automatically fix things. It doesn't end the struggle. Sometimes it just changes the scenery for the battle. The fear and worry fight is a daily one for me. Actually, and unfortunately, more than daily. But I've learned it helps if I remind myself of two things when it comes to fighting fear and worry.

One, is this: the other shoe is going to drop.

I know, it's difficult. But, we all know it's true. This life is full of disappointment, hardships, and trial. No one is exempt. There are going to be some falling shoes, Chicken Little. You're just going to have to accept that fact and be thankful it's not the entire sky.

But, as depressing as the first point is, the second point helps.

Two, I believe in and serve an Almighty God who never allows a "shoe to drop" without it passing through his sovereign, merciful hands.

We're getting into some deep theology here. We're opening the discussion about God allowing evil and pain. That's a tough one. Why would He do such a thing?

I'm not a theologian. I have a simple mind and a simple faith. And so if you're looking for mind-blowing intellect, you're reading the wrong book. I've already referenced Chicken Little, the Road Runner, and Wile E. Coyote in this section. Hardly John Wesley-level thinking. But, what I do have is a relationship with the God of this universe. I know Him. I don't claim to understand Him completely, but, I do know what He says to be true about Himself.

God is the inventor of love and life. He's the one who thought them up. He then put them into practice by creating us. He loves us. Truly. Deeply. Enough to give us life.

But we, us stinking humans, brought sin into this world by our own free will and choosing, and through a couple who just couldn't keep their little hands off a piece of forbidden fruit. Before we speak too harshly about Adam and Eve, let's remember we probably would have been the ones to do it if it had been us in that garden. I won't speak for you, but I know I'm a rotten sinner, I don't even need a forbidden fruit tree to prove it.

When sin entered the world, the world broke. It wasn't created for sin and death. Sin leads to death and death just doesn't sit well with us. I think that's why death hurts so much. It wasn't supposed to be that way. We weren't created for death.

But with sin and death come tragedies and pain. A lot of shoes have fallen throughout history and they have caused significant damage.

Now God, who is perfect, is still in control. That's what He tells us in His Word. Romans 8 is a good place to start reading if you want to see what He said about this through the apostle Paul.

God could stop every shoe from falling this very second if He wanted to. But instead, He allows them to pass through His sovereign hands. Why? Well, I can't answer that completely. But, I do know those shoes, and their ensuing pain, have led me closer to God and have helped me to recognize my need for Him. The pain and hurt remind us that we live in a broken world that is not our home. A quote credited to C.S. Lewis (see, I can discuss theology without using cartoon references) says, "The fact that our heart yearns for something Earth can't supply is proof that Heaven must be our home."

As foreigners in this broken world, we long for home. At least we should. Maybe sometimes God uses those awful shoes that fall to help us yearn for Him. Like I said, I can't explain it all, but I believe it. And I find comfort in it.

When I find myself in fear and worry mode (more often than I'd like to admit) and realize I'm missing life because I'm holding my breath and listening for the impact of a falling shoe, I remember point number two. God is still in control. He is only going to allow what He knows is good and perfect in His sovereign way. I don't know how He does it, but I trust Him.

Furthermore, I think about the fact that God allowed a gigantic shoe to fall on His own Son, Jesus. Perhaps now I'm taking this analogy a bit too far. Can't you just hear the preschoolers telling their mommies and daddies that Jesus was squashed by a giant sandal? Crushed by a sole to save my soul? On a hill far away stood an old rugged Croc? I digress.

Let me start over with this point.

God allowed His own Son, Jesus, to be murdered by the very people He created. God allowed horrible things to happen to His Son on our behalf. God allowed Jesus, who had no sin, to suffer because of our sin. He did this so that those of us who believe, repent, and accept His sacrifice can someday live eternally in a world without pain. That's the gospel, folks. It really is that simple.

What's more, in the meantime, before we experience the wonder of God's presence in Heaven, we have His presence with us here on Earth. God's faithfulness, provision, unconditional love, mercy, grace, and hope are always available to me. Now. Today! By choosing to acknowledge and accept them, I can start to conquer that stupid worry and fear. I can thaw out from the frozen stances of waiting for a shoe to drop, and instead move and blink again. I can live! I can even take a deep breath knowing that no matter what shoe drops, God is in control, and He will be with me through it.

I don't know when the next shoe will hit the ground near me. I hope it's a flip-flop or something light, but I don't get to make that choice. I do, however, get to choose how I'll live in the meantime.

Am I going to waste my time worrying about the future and being frozen with fear, or am I going to live joyfully and fully while trusting in my Sovereign Lord?

I know, I know. It's easy to say, and much more difficult to live. I understand. I'm right there with you in the trenches trying to make this trust a habit in my every moment. I'm desperately working to replace worry and fear with peace and joy. I certainly haven't perfected it, but I'm nothing if not persistent. I'm going to keep at it. We can do this together.

A boy's dress shoe began this mental dialogue and had such a profound impact on my thinking. In the future, I hope that's the only place Karson's shoes make impact!

*   *   *

Nothing to Lose
Originally posted on *Ten Blue Eyes* blog, June 21, 2016

I'll never forget what she said. She stood behind the simple podium telling a room full of young moms the heartbreaking story of her infant daughter's death. My throat grew tight and many eyes filled with tears as she told our MOPS (Mothers of Preschoolers) group the details of her unimaginable loss. But one statement in particular hit me. And it stuck. Though it has been years since that morning, I have replayed her words in my head often, as if she said them just last week.

She said something like:

"This may sound strange, but now that we have other children and I try every day to protect them from this world and to raise them right, there are times when I'm thankful that the daughter that we lost is already safe. Nothing can harm her now. She's with the Heavenly Father, and she's safe."

Her transparency is capable of encouraging many others to live with such a perspective. Her worldview is an eternal one. Her hope is not rooted on Earth, but in Heaven. Her trust is in an invisible and loving God.

Though she has lost the most precious thing, she has nothing to lose.

I know for a fact that this woman would have rather not faced her horrific pain in order to gain such a mature and godly perspective. But we don't always have a choice in our life lesson plan. We do however have a choice in how we'll accept it.

Her words remind me to accept an eternal perspective.

That with our Heavenly Father's love and the gift of hope He offers, we have everything to gain.

And when we rest in the Truth, we have nothing to lose.

"He is no fool who gives what he cannot keep to gain what he cannot lose." Jim Elliot

*   *   *

We stood in the middle of the mall, the aroma of soft pretzels tempting us, and we watched. Some strangers, a mother and her three children, were dropping coins into a big donation funnel. Technically, they're called hyperbolic funnels, but often they have names such as Coin Vortex or Funnel of Love. This one was red, and I don't remember where the coins were being donated. I was more impressed with the process.

It doesn't matter how many times I've seen it, I always find it satisfying to stop and watch the coins. A hand places them in the little slot at the outside edge of the funnel, and lets go. The coin then makes a wide, circular loop around the large circumference of the funnel. Slowly and gradually it makes a path on a smaller looping circle. Round and round it goes, getting closer to the center with each moment, yet taking its time to cover a lot of ground. Finally, when it gets to the very center, its movements speed up because the circle is now much smaller. Spin. Spin. Spin. Spin. Spin. Drop.

The coin falls into the belly of the funnel and is safe until the powers-that-be remove them to donate to the selected charity.

When thinking about my approach to worry, I can largely relate to this plastic funnel. A thought will enter my head. Then the thought will make a wide looping pass through my brain. And then it goes around again. And again.

And again.

I want to slam my hand down on the worry and stop it in its tracks, but I can't seem to catch up with it. I can't seem to get rid of it that quickly.

Then there's my husband. His approach to worry is more like that of a coin fountain. You take the coin. You throw the coin into the water. Plunk. It's over.

I'm happy for him, but as a funnel worrier, fountain worriers can be a little annoying. I'm just saying.

At times, I'd really like to discuss my worry with Kraig. If I have a coin that has been rolling around for a while, and it still has plenty of steam until it plunks, I need to process it verbally, and so I bring it up to Kraig. The following example may or may not have been an actual worry I've had. Okay, it is. Stop judging me.

"You've been really sore and tight in your neck and shoulders lately," I say to Kraig as he's sitting in the other recliner in the family room. He looks up at me with no expression. "What if there's a tumor or something in your neck pushing on nerves? Should you go get it checked out?"

His expression remains very apathetic. He's mentally picking up his coin of worry and preparing to toss it into ... oh wait! He's already tossed it! It's gone, folks. Sunk to the bottom of his worry fountain.

"I'm fine," he says. "I think I've just got some tight muscles."

My coin is still rolling. Rollin', rollin', rollin'. See that worry rollin'.

How can he so quickly and easily get rid of the worry coin? And why can't he understand that my worry coin is nowhere near dropping yet? Can't he empathize with my spinning mind instead of watching his coin hit the fountain at breakneck speed?

We funnel worriers need a fix. We need some tricks to help us get those worry coins to drop faster. How can we make it a piece of cake to simply not worry as often?

For one, saying the worry out loud helps. It can be very embarrassing, and we will want to be mindful of whom we choose to share with, but usually, my fountain worrier husband is a good choice for me. I've found, over the years of our marriage, that he doesn't always understand my funnel worrying, but that doesn't matter. He's able to expedite my worry coin's trip.

Sometimes, what he says in response to my spoken worries will act as a hand smacking the coin and stopping it right there. Other times, his response will help me move the worry to its resting place quicker. Kraig doesn't think less of me because of these conversations. We simply have learned that we each have our own approach. I'd like to be able to state that one approach is not better than another, but I'm afraid that wouldn't be true. I do think one approach is better. His.

Grrr.

I believe that as Christians, we are taught not to worry. In fact, Jesus addressed worry very specifically in a sermon. Matthew 6 records Jesus' Sermon on the Mount, and worry is one of its topics. And do you know what Jesus says about worry? Don't do it.

"Therefore I tell you, do not worry about your life." (Matthew 6:25)

Do not worry.

So it seems to me, that if Jesus addressed worry as something we shouldn't do, then worry will be something that we naturally are tempted to do. Otherwise, He wouldn't have mentioned it.

So we're all tempted to worry. It's a part of being a human.

But, if Jesus is telling us not to worry, then we need to listen.

It would seem that the fountain worrier has an advantage over the funnel worrier. The fountain worrier is able to dismiss the worry much faster than the funnel worrier. Therefore, less time is spent worrying and more time is spent being obedient to Jesus.

But by nature, I'm a funnel worrier. I want to obey. I want to stop the worries faster, but I have to work at it. And working at something in order to be more obedient to God is a spiritual act of worship. It's a beautiful thing. If you look at it that way, we funnel worriers have an advantage—we spend more time practicing being obedient in this area. Maybe we're the winners after all?

But, let's not make everything a competition, shall we?

So, as we funnel worriers are using our time learning to ditch worries when those coins start rolling, we need some tools.

What tools can we use to work on this? How can we turn our ugly worry funnels into beautiful fountains?

As we've already discussed, verbalizing the worry to a safe person is a good practice.

Two, we can replace the worry with a truth. Jesus models this for us in His sermon. He says,

> Look at the birds of the air; they do not sow or reap or store away in barns, and yet your heavenly Father feeds them. Are you not much more valuable than they? Can any one of you by worrying add a single hour to your life? And why do you worry about clothes? See how the flowers of the field grow. They do not labor or spin. Yet I tell you that not even Solomon in all his splendor was dressed like one of these. If that is how God clothes the grass of the field, which is here today and tomorrow is thrown into the fire, will he not much more clothe you—you of little faith? So do not worry, saying, "What shall we eat?" or "What shall we drink?" or "What shall we wear?" For the pagans run after all these things, and your heavenly Father knows that you need them.

It's too bad the natural acoustics on the mountainside negated the need for a sound system, because Jesus could have done a nice mic drop here.

The truth is, God is in control of all life. The birds, the flowers, the grass. He knows our needs better than we know them ourselves, and He will take care of us according to His sovereign will.

I love how He asks who of us by worrying can add a single hour to our lives. Sometimes my own pride runs so rampant and awful that I may have been the one in the crowd crinkling up my nose and slowly raising my hand. "Uh. Maybe I can, Jesus. Have you heard about this whole clean eating thing? I may be able to boost my own immune system. That could add some days. Hours at the least!"

Oh, my goodness! How foolish of me! How plain stupid to think my worrying has any positive function whatsoever! It does not.

23

In case you think that proactive worrying is a good practice, let me tell you, I've tried it, and it doesn't work either.

What is proactive worrying? Some of you fountain worriers are so blissfully naïve. You see, there's this idea that by worrying about something that hasn't happened yet, you'll have worried enough to prepare yourself so that when the actual bad event occurs, it won't be as awful.

But it doesn't work. Unfortunately, I've found that it just wastes the good times before the bad event happened, and now you've had to worry twice as much.

I can't believe I'm going to tell you this, but when I was a kid, I used to lie in bed at night and quietly say, "excuse me," over and over. I thought if I said it enough times, and sort of banked the "excuse mes", then I wouldn't have to say it when I burped in the future. I honestly have no idea where I got this notion, but it turns out I wasted some good pre-sleep time as a kid where I could have been daydreaming about the next Babysitter's Club book or something else fancy like that.

As silly as that sounds, worrying is just as silly.

So, fellow funnel worriers, verbalize those dumb worries. Verbalize the ones that don't feel dumb, but that feel real and heavy too. And then, replace them with a truth.

I often ask myself, "What do I know to be true?" It helps me stop the rolling worry coin, or at the very least it helps me get it to drop sooner.

"Do I have any evidence right now that Kraig has a tumor in his neck other than the stiffness he feels?"

No.

"Does it make sense that Kraig may just have tight muscles?"

Yes.

"Is it very likely that Kraig has a tumor?"

No.

And the worry coin is falling away.

To help stop worry, think about what you know to be true. The other thoughts that are not true can be peeled away and thrown into the trash. Adiós, untrue thoughts! You have no purpose here.

I'm not sure I've torn down my worry funnel yet. It's got yellow caution tape around it because it's under construction, but it's not gone. Unfortunately, sometimes I find it to still be very functional. But, I'm really working on being a fountain worrier. I'm speaking those awful worries aloud to Kraig or to a trusted friend. I'm replacing those worry lies with truths.

Sometimes I open my Bible to verses such as Job 42:2.

"I know you can do all things. No plan of yours can be thwarted."

Job said this to God. Job had lost all ten of his children and almost all of his earthly possessions in one day. Enough loss to create some serious PTSD. I would have been prone to major worry and anxiety after such calamity. But, Job states his belief and trust in God's power and sovereignty. He says God can't be thrown for a loop. This was a comfort for Job, and it is to me as well.

I also think about Proverbs 16:9.

"In their hearts humans plan their course, but the Lord establishes their steps."

I can think and worry all I want, but ultimately, I believe God is in control.

The truths from Scripture soothe me. They help me regain perspective and they are wonderful replacements to the irrational thoughts and lies that were using up cranium space.

Speaking the worries aloud. Replacing them with truths.

It's helping. It really is.

The beautiful work of learning to obey Jesus' words is producing a fountain of peace inside my worry-weary soul.

*   *   *

Slice of Hope: When we share our worries with a trusted friend, and replace our anxiety with what we know to be true, we can begin to live in the peace which Jesus daily provides.

two

guilt and regret

That's How the Cookie Crumbles

Originally posted on *Ten Blue Eyes* blog, October 29, 2013

If I'd had an interrogation room and a bright light, I would have used them. Instead, I parked my three-year-old daughter in a kitchen chair across from me. I wasn't about to let her big blue eyes and blonde pigtails fool me. This kid was guilty. And she was going down for it. Today, Mommy was playing prosecutor, judge and jury. Court was in session.

The crime? Oh, it may sound trivial, but that wasn't the point. I didn't care about the Hershey Kiss that had disappeared off the top of the peanut butter cookie. I cared about the *truth*. All I wanted was a confession so that this kid could learn her lesson, be forgiven, and move on toward better obedience.

The gavel had been banging in my brain and the evidence lay nearby on the counter. The container of cookies was mostly full, but when I had lifted the lid, one of the chocolate kisses was gone, leaving a little round dent in the sugary peanut butter dough.

The defendant sat swinging her little legs as I paced the kitchen floor. I began to present my case.

I had clearly instructed Karly to stay out of the cookies. She had asked, she'd been given an answer, and she had defiantly disobeyed by taking that little chocolate morsel. And she thought she'd get away with it too.

Karly kept claiming that she was innocent. But, oh, she was not.

Had she been able to read and write I would have, at this point, slid a piece of paper and a pen in front of her and asked her to write out her confession. But I was going to have to settle for a verbal explanation. So I sat down and waited.

Did I ever hear a story.

In her sweet, high-pitched little voice, Karly told me that I had it all wrong. She was being framed. A bird took the candy.

A bird?

Her plea continued as she explained that a bird had, in fact, flown into the kitchen through the window over the sink, taken the Hershey Kiss, put the lid back on the cookie tub and then proceeded to fly out the same way it entered.

Mind you this was in the middle of winter, when that window hadn't been opened in weeks.

That's it! The jury has made their decision and you, my dear little one, are guilty! You are guilty of disobeying, and now lying to, Mommy. I sighed deeply to show my frustration and disappointment.

At this point my husband entered the crime scene and was given a recap of events. He then walked over to the cookie tub and lifted the lid. After looking at the cookies for a moment he picked up the container and walked over to me. We looked inside together and there, stuck to the bottom of another cookie, was the missing Hershey Kiss.

The bird had been exonerated.

I looked over at the adorable little defendant. She had been proven innocent as well.

What had I done? I had been so focused on getting what I thought was the truth from her that she had made up a story to appease me.

Judge Judy is going to love this one.

Case dismissed. But now I was the one who had some explaining to do.

I sat across from Karly and told her that we had found the missing piece of candy. I told her that I knew a bird hadn't flown in and taken it, and that I now knew that she hadn't disobeyed and taken it either. I admitted to her that Mommy was wrong. I told her that I was really sorry.

She shrugged in that toddler way, and accepted my apology faster than she'd conjured up the bird story. She forgave me without a second thought and off she skipped without a care in her mind.

I stayed in that chair for awhile. Though the jury box and the courtroom were emptying out in my mind, regret nudged me. Why had I gotten so riled up over a Hershey Kiss? Why had I pushed Karly so hard for a confession that she had to make one up to calm me down? And how had she been able to forgive me so quickly and easily when she could have easily pointed an accusing finger right back in my face?

She forgave me because she's a little child. In her toddler mind, she wasn't out to get me or seek revenge. She could forget the offense in the blink of an eye and never bring it up again.

I took her to court that day, but she took me to school. I had been shown a great lesson in how to forgive and forget.

To this day, I can't look at a peanut butter cookie adorned with a Hershey Kiss without laughing about that crazy bird story. That's okay. It's good for me to be reminded now and then—that I'm not always right, even when I think I am. That sometimes I have to confess my mistakes and accept the forgiveness of others.

I hope I can forgive and forget in the same way Karly forgave me. I want to experience and offer forgiveness completely. Skipping away, as free as a bird!

*   *   *

Guilt. Another arch nemesis of mine.

Guilt shows itself often in my life. One arena in which it frequently opposes me? Motherhood.

When I became a mother, many advised me on a wide variety of topics. I also possessed a plethora of ideas and plans of my own. I did my best to prepare. I took a childbirth class at the hospital. I read books and magazines about every aspect of parenting, from breastfeeding to college savings funds. I believed I had a grip on what to expect from being a mom.

But I don't remember anyone ever warning me about the mom guilt.

Or maybe they did, and I forgot. Great, I failed to remember. Add another serving of mom guilt to the heap.

The mom guilt doesn't wait around to be invited, either. For me, she showed up early on, like a rude houseguest who has overstayed her welcome and is having mail forwarded to my address. What a parasite!

I've been a mom now for fourteen years. Not long enough to claim expertise (Ha! Not even close!), but long enough to gain some experience under the belt of my mom jeans. I've encountered mom guilt frequently.

Here is an incomplete list of instances during which I've experienced mom guilt in one form or another:

- Pregnancy

- Childbirth

- Hospital stay after childbirth

- The infanthoods of my children

- Breastfeeding

- Introducing solid foods

- Introducing non-organic table food

- Introducing doughnuts

- The toddlerhoods of my children

- Losing my cool with my toddlers due to my lack of sleep

- Losing my cool with my toddlers due to their lack of sleep

- Losing my cool with my toddlers due to their lack of toilet use

- Losing my cool with my toddlers due to my own lack of solo bathroom use

- The preschool years of my children

- Losing my cool with my preschoolers due to their lack of being adults

- The elementary years of my children

- Losing my cool with my elementary children due to spelling tests

- Losing my cool with my elementary children due to the state of their bedrooms

- The middle school years of my children

Etcetera. The only reason this list does not go on? My children haven't hit the high school years yet. Guilt about their futures sometimes attacks me, but I just don't have the wherewithal to extend the list to future mom guilt right now. The past and present mom guilt is enough to sustain me.

Let's dig deeper into this topic of mom guilt, and hopefully redeem it in some way. Let me expound upon one area from my list.

- Losing my cool with my elementary children due to the state of their bedrooms

"Losing my cool" has been defined differently by mothers for generations. June Cleaver probably felt guilt and thought she'd lost her cool over saying, "Oh, Beaver!" while Wilma Flintstone apparently never lost any sleep over the fact that she couldn't find a shirt long enough to cover Pebbles' torso. We all deal with different types of mom guilt, and different levels of subsequent reactions.

My personality is fairly laid-back and mellow. I am not an overly aggressive or angry person (unless I'm playing balloon volleyball with my children, and we'll get to that in a later chapter). I am, by nature, not a big reactor. In fact, I'm certain I'd never hear "Christy Cabe, come on down!" from my hypothetical audience chair at *The Price Is Right* game show. I've been told they watch the audience members, and then choose people who will react in a big, fun way when their names are called. The show looks for the screamers, the crazy shirt-wearers, and those who will flap their arms and jump up and down when they win a new car. My name would never be called.

In high school or college, I was sitting at my grandma's table enjoying a snack, while Grandma worked in the kitchen. When she opened a cupboard where the dishes had been stacked at an unfortunate angle, they fell out with a crash. I slowly turned around in my chair and looked.

Grandma shook her head and said, "You didn't even react! You are so laid-back!" I wondered what I should have done. Screamed? Fallen off my chair? Helped pick up the dishes? Yes, probably that last one.

So, when I say I lose my cool, it may look different than another mom losing her cool.

Let's define "losing our cool" as any time we, as mothers, feel disappointed in our responses to our children. You know, those times when we wish for a do-over. Another great word for it would be "regret." Regret is a very close cousin to guilt. An ugly cousin.

Regretting how you've lost your cool with your child can look different from one mom to the next, or from one day to the next. Perhaps you've yelled. Maybe you've said something unkind under your breath. You've intentionally ignored your child or thrown his gaming system into the street. Perhaps you just were not as supportive as you could have been.

It's all about the disappointment, because just as a boat leaves a wake, mom guilt leaves us wallowing in a trail of disappointment.

My daughters' bedroom remains my own mom-guilt kryptonite. My girls share a fairly large room, and an affinity for messiness. They overachieve at filling every nook and cranny with junk.

I have intentionally made it a goal of mine to make our house a home where everyone feels comfortable living. I don't want my children, husband, or our guests, to feel like we live in a museum and that they cannot touch things. I also do not wish to strive for perfection. However, I do like things to be neat. Stress decreases when it doesn't look like a bomb just went off in the living room.

So, I try very hard to balance my love of neatness with my daughters' love of disarray. Actually, I think they just don't really care either way. Sometimes apathy is the nastiest enemy.

Periodically, I will go into their bedroom and we will have a "talk."

We will discuss my desire to be understanding, and to not hold them to a standard of perfection. Then we will discuss my expectations and how they can better meet them. Then they will complain about the other one and how the mess was mostly their "sister's fault." Then we will begin cleaning the room together. Then my blood pressure rises and I begin the transformation into the Incredible Hulk. Purple cut-off shorts and muscles and everything! I say things I shouldn't. I resort to sarcasm. "Oh, you knew that shirt was under your bed for three months. You were keeping it there on purpose! So brilliant of you!"

By the time we're done cleaning, my girls feel wounded and I feel horrible for hurting them.

Oh, hey there, Regret. I see you've come to join the struggle.

I cool down. I apologize. They forgive me. They throw the clean laundry I've just folded onto the floor.

It is a battle. Not just the bedroom mess, but the fight I have over my own reaction and subsequent disappointment. I'm sick of feeling disappointed with myself.

I've forgotten to send birthday treats to school with my son. I've allowed my kids to eat too much candy. I've yelled at them. I've belittled them. I've held them to unrealistic expectations. I've literally fallen down while holding one of them, and I've accidently caused them physical pain. I've failed in many moments of mothering.

Mom guilt has stung me more times than I can count.

I know I'm not alone. After releasing my book, *Brownie Crumbs*, and speaking more than forty times that first year it was out, I found some fellow mom-guilt-sufferers in the moms' groups where I spoke. I shared about the failed philosophy of mom guilt, that we mothers should be perfect, and then offered practical ways we could combat it. My favorite moment of mom-guilt camaraderie came when one group of moms did an icebreaker called "Mom Guilt Bingo." They handed out Bingo cards with squares that read, "Used TV As Babysitter," "High Fructose Corn Syrup in the Home," "Had An Epidural," "Forgot to Play Tooth Fairy." Then these moms went around the room and signed each other's Bingo boards in the boxes where they had, in fact, suffered such a "failure." It was a riot! They understood mom guilt and even laughed in her ugly face.

I enjoy laughing over moments of mom guilt, especially when they're not my own! We all love reading posts on social media about other moms who fail. The birthday cakes that are supposed to look like cute little Minions from *Despicable Me*, but instead look like a scud missile in overalls. The kids that were left alone for too long and are now covered head-to-toe in Sharpie. The babies that fall out of strollers or swings or roll down a hill because they weren't safely secured. It's truly heartwarming to see. When we know no one was hurt, that is, other than Mom's pride. It feels so good to know we're not alone.

Mom guilt can also be "grandmothered in."

My mother-in-law had given my youngest daughter a shirt for Christmas with the poop emoji on the front and the word #SUPER. When Kenzie opened the gift, I laughed and asked my mother-in-law if she knew that she'd given her granddaughter a shirt with poop on it. She looked confused and said she'd thought it was soft-serve ice cream. We laughed, and Kenzie added the shirt to her repertoire. Then Kenzie inadvertently wore it to school on spring picture day! She was embarrassed, and so she put her jacket on and zipped it up for the photo. The photo turned out quite lovely. And so did the memory. We never buy the spring school photos anyway. Why not wear a shirt with number two on it for the second picture day of the year?

My mother-in-law could have experienced "Grandma Guilt," but she instead laughed and enjoyed the moment.

I believe we should laugh in the face of mom guilt! To strip her of some of her power. To take away some of her poise and to reclaim our own dignity.

When I was a younger mom and attending a MOPS (Mothers of Preschoolers) group at my church, I remember the speaker talking about disciplining our children. She spoke specifically about very young children who were still learning about boundaries. She said that if they were, for example, playing with something breakable from the coffee table and you told them to put it back and not touch it, that we should give them a moment to respond. We should take a deep breath. Wait. Allow them the time to process, make their decision, and execute it. She said we should not take away their dignity by making the decision too quickly for them by ripping it out of their hand and putting it back where we wanted it. Or, by lecturing them they should do the correct thing. No, we tell them, we wait. We give them a chance to make the best choice. We encourage them for their successes, and teach them kindly and gently after their failures. We help protect their dignity.

Why can't we treat ourselves the same way?

I've tried to allow my kids to make their own decisions and live with the consequences. What's even more difficult, I've tried to learn to live with my own consequences. To protect my own dignity. To lift my chin and straighten my crown.

I am going to fail. I am going to make the wrong decisions sometimes. I am going to hurt my children's feelings. I am going to teach them incorrectly. I am going to wish I could call a do-over.

But that is okay. I can forgive myself. I can try to do better the next time. I can even laugh about it in the here and now.

That takes the sting out of mom guilt.

Mom guilt is a jerk. Regret is her accomplice. They've threatened to ruin some precious moments, and have often succeeded. But thankfully, I know someone more dignified and powerful. Grace.

Grace takes down Guilt and Regret every time we allow her to. Sometimes it's a real wrestling match. Headlocks and squirming and screaming and moaning included. But battles worth fighting are often ugly ones.

In the midst of all of that, we can show dignity like a royal butler and, with a grand sweep of our arms, usher Grace into the moment. Even if the moment looks a lot like a boxing ring.

Come on in, Grace. You are welcome here. Please have your mail forwarded to this address.

*   *   *

Okay, okay. You've welcomed Grace in. She's made herself comfortable. She knows where the bath towels are and how to find the cereal in the morning (or cake if she prefers). But now what? How do you actually allow Grace to beat up Guilt and Regret?

Unfortunately, it's not a one-time battle. It may be fought in a boxing ring, or in your kitchen, or in your children's bedrooms, or in the deepest, most secret parts of your soul. It doesn't really matter the battlefield. Wherever it is fought, it's an all-out war. And it is going to rage on forever. Or at least for as long as you're drawing breath into your lungs. It's a constant striving to help Grace win. She can succeed, mind you. She's bigger than Guilt and Regret, but you have to allow her some space to move and work. But how?

Gosh, I wish I knew.

Honestly, how can I even sit here and write about something such as allowing Grace to beat Guilt and Regret when I can hear them screaming at each other and tearing up the house behind me? I have not signed the peace treaty on this war yet. I never will. How am I a qualified general to give orders?

But perhaps that is what makes my words even more heartfelt. Because I'm in this war with you. I'm sleeping in the stinking tents. I'm eating the rations. I've got beads of sweat rolling down my back. I get it.

So, though I do not claim expertise or victory, I do know what it's like to fight Guilt and Regret. And I want to share some battle tactics with you.

First, start with your mind. Think about what you know to be true.

Now wait, you say. That sounds like the same advice you were dishing out earlier when it came to worry. Now you're giving us the exact same piece of wisdom to deal with guilt? This is cheap.

Thank you for your concern. Yes, I am giving you the same advice again. Do you know why? Because *it works!* This is a two-for-one deal, and I am not even going to ask you to pay for this book twice. You're welcome.

When guilt creeps into my mind, I have a tendency to let it take up residency for awhile. I replay the moment that led to my guilt. I watch it again and again in my mind's eye hoping that maybe I will see it from an angle that makes me feel less guilty, when actually the opposite usually occurs. I feel worse. A good way to stop the guilt replay is to instead think about what I know to be true.

My youngest child, Kenzie, injured her wrist by falling off a skateboard. She had to wear a brace and a sling on her left arm full-time for six weeks. Thankfully, she's right-handed, so it was her "off arm," but it still inconvenienced her. She handled it like a champ, and I made sure to tell her often how proud I was of how she was adjusting to being one-armed. Mom guilt pretty much stayed out of this situation, other than a little twinge I felt over not taking her to see the doctor for three days after the fall. It was understandable that we did not know the extent of the injury. No bones were sticking out of skin, or anything crazy like that. So, I had mostly let the guilt go, and I had moved on with feeling guilty in other areas of life.

Then one day after school, Kenzie pulled her folder out of her backpack and handed me a stack of papers. I flipped through them while half-listening to something Karly was trying to tell me about her day. And then I saw Kenzie's spelling test. She had misspelled some of the words. Words that we had practiced together multiple times the week before, and words she knew how to spell. Upon closer inspection, it looked like a toddler had taken this test. Or maybe an orangutan. The handwriting was atrocious! (No offense to the toddlers or primates who may be reading this.)

"Kenzie! What is the deal here?" I whined. "Why did you write so sloppy and why did you misspell these words? You knew them when we practiced!"

Her little face fell and she sunk deeper into her chair at the kitchen table. "Mom, I can't hold the paper still when I write because of my sling! It was sliding all around and I couldn't make the letters any neater! And, I don't know why I missed them. I was just really upset!" She started to cry.

Stick a fork in me. I'm done with my line of questioning. Of course she couldn't hold the paper still with her left hand. Of course she was dealing with more stress then she was letting on. Of course she gets flustered like the rest of the human race and sometimes can't remember the most basic of information when under pressure. Of course she's in second grade and allowed to not know how to spell certain words. Heck, a lot of words!

I apologized and hugged her and told her again how proud I was of the little lady she was becoming. But my heart hurt for a while. I replayed the scene again and again in my mind that evening.

Finally, I decided I needed to let go of the guilt. I used the truth method. What do I know to be true?

Did I intentionally try to hurt Kenzie's feelings? No.

Has Kenzie seemed to be affected by my careless comments more than just her initial reaction? No.

Have I, in all probability, hurt Kenzie so deeply with my words that she will now turn to illegal drugs tomorrow? No.

Have I ruined the English language for Kenzie for the rest of her life? Probably not.

Of course these questions are a little silly. But when I really think about how much I believe my failures can negatively affect someone's life, particularly small missteps like this example, I realize it is all somewhat silly. Let's be realistic. Most of the things we feel guilty about are small missteps. The big no-nos that should produce guilt, like never speaking a kind word to your child in their lifetime, locking them in a closet, only feeding them bread crumbs, or forcing them to watch horror movies at the age of three, are probably not happening in your home. That is why they make TV shows about such things, because they are rare and horrific and draw viewers, not because they are common. Let's relax a little and remember that we are doing okay.

We parents think too much of ourselves if we think we alone hold our child's potential for success so tightly and precisely in our grip. We are here to help the birds fly out of the nest, but we are not going to be moving their wings up and down for them with our white knuckled hands. No, we're gently shooing them with those hands. And to shoo them, we need to let go of them.

We take far too much credit for both the good and the bad. There are other family members, friends, teachers, youth workers, and even other kids that will impact and influence your child whether you parent perfectly or not. So let's ease up on the guilt a bit. It's not all about us.

I am not suggesting we throw all caution to the wind and forget even trying. Don't literally throw the baby, or the pimply preteen, out with the bathwater. Let's keep the children, and let's keep mothering them to the best of our abilities. Are we going to make mistakes? You bet. Are we going to have some really great moments too? Absolutely!

What do I know to be true? I know that I love my children so much that sometimes I physically feel a tingle run through my body when I check on them after they've fallen asleep. I know I want the very best for them. I know that I do not want to spare them every disappointment or pain because I want them to learn to deal with those things on their own. I know I don't want them to be living with me when they're thirty and still be asking me to help them study for their spelling tests. Hello? Have you heard of spell-check, Honey?

These things that I know trump the feelings of guilt. So it looks like Truth is a good fighter to send into battle when Guilt and Regret begin to rear their ugly heads.

Then there's Forgiveness. Forgiveness doesn't work alone. At least I've not found much success with releasing her to fly solo. Forgiveness likes to go into battle hand-in-hand with Grace. Good ol' Grace. Remember her? She's the one we welcomed in to start this whole guilt resistance training in the first place.

Forgiveness and Grace work so well together. They deliver the old one-two punch.

When I have a moment of mom guilt that is weighing me down, and I'm replaying it and feeling awful about it, I can first think about what I know to be true. That will set me on the right track toward recovery. Then, I should make sure I've sought forgiveness. First, I need to ask my child/children for their forgiveness. It is so freeing and wonderful to admit to your children that you're wrong. It sets the stage for the future of your parenting and lowers the expectations. Your children will soon learn and accept that their parent is not perfect. Even that little bit of truth will allow them to accept their own failures with more grace.

After apologizing to your children, and (hopefully) receiving their forgiveness, you need to forgive one other very important person. Yourself.

Forgive yourself. Here are some highly motivational statements you may want to print out and hang on your wall. You are not really as great as you think you are. You will mess up. You will fail. You are not always going to get it right. You are a human being (unless you are one of those orangutans reading this book, and if so, my apologies once again).

We need to learn to forgive ourselves. I need to learn to forgive myself. And that is where Grace comes in. Grace is what makes Forgiveness really kick into beast mode. Grace makes Forgiveness possible.

There are a variety of definitions of the word "Grace" if you look them up in the dictionary (does anyone actually still own a dictionary)? But, I noticed that in almost every one, the word "unmerited" is used. Unmerited means undeserved. Grace is not something we deserve or earn. That would be a wage, or a paycheck, or a good swift kick in the pants. Grace can't be earned. That is what is so amazing about it.

You know I love the Bible, and I find that when I truly study it, it teaches me things that I can apply today. Like right now. Even about mom guilt!

There are two particular passages I read together recently that opened my eyes. They deal with employing grace and forgiveness, and as I've mentioned, that is a great tactic for defeating guilt.

The first passage is found in 2 Samuel 9. This is in the Old Testament, before Jesus lived on earth, and it's talking about Israel's king, David.

David had a best friend, Jonathan, who was the son of David's enemy, Saul. Now, Saul literally tried to pin David against a wall with a spear. More than once. (1 Samuel 18:11, 19:10, 20:33) Saul had anger issues. He particularly used his anger against David. Anyway, David forgave Saul (long story!), and loved Saul's son, Jonathan, as his best friend. Now, fast forward years after the spear-throwing thing, and David is now king, and his enemy and best friend have died in battle.

David says, in 2 Samuel 9:1, "Is there anyone still left of the house of Saul to whom I can show kindness for Jonathan's sake?"

It turns out a crippled son of Jonathan's still lives in the kingdom. David finds out about this guy, whose name is Mephibosheth (what a tough name to learn to spell in kindergarten!), and he brings him to the palace. David tells Mephibosheth he is going to treat him as his own heir, and gives him a seat at the king's table for every meal.

Mephibosheth isn't so sure about this. He says, "What is your servant, that you should notice a dead dog like me?"

Good question, Mephi (can I call you Mephi?) Why would the king show such kindness?

1 Samuel 9:7 says, "Don't be afraid," David said to him, "for I will surely show you kindness for the sake of your father Jonathan. I will restore to you all the land that belonged to your grandfather Saul, and you will always eat at my table."

This was employing grace, folks. David showed grace, unearned favor, to a guy to whom he had no real obligation. He did this because he loved Jonathan, and because he forgave Saul. He ultimately did this because he loved and served God!

David employed grace and forgiveness by showing kindness. These things helped ease the pain of the past. They defeated the broken and ugly pattern.

Now, if you will, look with me at a New Testament passage. This is after Jesus has lived, died, resurrected, and ascended. This is a passage written by Paul to the Ephesians. Paul explains Jesus' finished work to them. He's explaining grace. Ephesians 2:4-7 reads,

> But because of his great love for us, God, who is rich in mercy, made us alive with Christ even when we were dead in transgressions—it is by grace you have been saved. And God raised us up with Christ and seated us with him in the heavenly realms in Christ Jesus, in order that in the coming ages he might show the incomparable riches of his grace, expressed in his kindness to us in Christ Jesus.

I am seeing some cool parallels here to the Mephi story. Just as Mephi saw himself as a "dead dog," we were all dead in our sins. Then, our King, Jesus, showed grace to us by giving us a seat at the table. We don't deserve it, but if we've accepted it, He seated us with him in the heavenly realms!

And, the last verse of the passage above says it was grace expressed in kindness. Unearned favor! Wow! Just like David showed Mephi a place in the kingdom as an act of kindness to show grace and forgiveness, Jesus did the same for me! For you! This gives me chills!

Grace, Forgiveness, Kindness. They defeat sin. They cover up ugly past. They defeat the broken patterns of sin, and help us to live and focus on Truth today.

They defeat that ugly ol' Guilt and Regret too.

I will face them again. Like I said, they are arch nemeses of mine.

But, it's not a lost cause! Grace and Forgiveness, Truth, and even simple Kindness can swoop in and fight for me, if I allow them to. I can't earn their help. I can't set up automatic monthly payments. I just have to accept it.

The victory dinner at the King's table is worth the effort!

*   *   *

My Summer (Guilt) Trip

Originally posted on *Ten Blue Eyes* blog, August 14, 2015

The lobby of the dorm where we'd been staying as a family during the summer camp my husband was directing was loud and crowded.

Teenagers laughed and chatted in little groups as they played cards, took selfies, and ate the ice cream sandwiches provided as the official late night snack before the mandatory "lights out" in a few minutes.

My own children, too young to be campers themselves, were having a heyday staying up past their bedtimes and playing with the "cool kids." My ten-year-old son was being trained in how to make the best paper airplane. My six-year-old daughter was following a group of teen girls around like a baby duckling following its mama, and my youngest child, five-year-old Kenzie, was sitting across the room from me.

I focused on Kenzie.

She sat on a little bench next to a woman she'd just met two days before, the camp nurse. I had just met this woman as well and had enjoyed the few conversations we'd had. Now as I watched Kenzie from across the noisy lobby I was intrigued. Kenzie, who is normally quiet around people she doesn't know well, looked as if she had launched into an animated dialogue. Her little mouth and hands were both moving rapidly, though I couldn't hear anything she was saying. I was curious to know what she was sharing with such gusto.

I had some guesses.

She was probably telling her new friend all about our fun summer as a family. How we'd been to the lake for vacation, traveled to a State Park, and had gone to Pennsylvania to visit family on what she thought was an adventure in the mountains. We had enjoyed so much time together this summer, the five of us, playing cards and swimming and laughing. I couldn't wait to hear what highlights Kenzie had shared.

I threw away the empty ice cream sandwich boxes and made my way through the adolescent mob to Kenzie and the nurse.

"I don't know what all Kenzie has been telling you, but it sure looked like you've been having quite the conversation over here!"

The kind woman shook her head. I waited with a smile on my face to hear which wonderful family memory Kenzie had let her in on.

"Kenzie was just telling me that you have so much work to do, that you sometimes can't even play Barbies with her."

The smile on my face slowly allowed gravity to pull it downward.

It took me a moment to grab onto this new train of thought and pull myself up into the rattling freight car that was whizzing down a completely different track than I was expecting.

And though I hadn't expected to be on this train, I certainly recognized it. I knew where it was headed.

All aboard, folks, we're on the fast track to Guilt Town. Mayor Mommy Guilt presiding.

I fumbled around with a few sentences saying something about the things kids say and then I sat down on the bench and changed the subject. Suddenly I needed to intensely watch the paper airplane seminar happening a few feet away from us. I wanted the planes to distract me from the crazy train of thought I was trying to disembark.

I have so much work to do?

I sometimes don't play Barbies with her?

Did she even tell her that sometimes I do play Barbies with her?

Did she happen to mention that I'm a stay-at-home Mom and I don't even go to work?

Apparently, my ticket to Guilt Town had been punched.

I felt guilty.

I didn't know if I *was* guilty, but I *felt* it all right.

With the title of "parent," a new skill set arrived. I can feel emotions at a whole new level. My emotions are blaring. Each noisy one seems to bring its ugly, uninvited opposite second-cousin once removed.

Elation shows up over chubby feet taking first steps and no sooner does it make itself comfortable, than Worry pushes through the door.

Joy seizes me as I watch a sweet face blow out birthday candles, but I suddenly find myself in the grip of Sadness as I realize that time is moving too quickly for me to savor.

Anticipation fills my mind as I send my child off to school, but soon Doubt waves its arms above its head trying to distract me from enjoying the moment.

Yes, I've had a lot of feelings as a mom. I've been all over the map. But I have to say that after frequenting many stops, I think I despise Guilt Town and its Mayor, "Mommy Guilt," the most.

I'd like to take that Mommy Guilt and ram my knee into her gut and then strangle her with my bare hands and roll her out to the curb.

And I'm not even a violent person.

She's a scoundrel. She's selfish and arrogant and let's face it, she's fat. She's a big fat liar.

Mommy Guilt likes to sneak up behind me and whisper things in my ear that cause me to doubt myself and what I know to be true. She can only focus on the negative. The lies. The doubts. The loss.

And I'm sick of her.

The paper airplane sailed in front of me derailing my train of thought.

I've got to get off this train. Not just now, but for good.

It seems to me that the best way to avoid a ride to Guilt Town is to intentionally go in another direction. Toward the truth.

I need to focus on what I know to be true.

Sometimes I don't play Barbies with my five-year-old.

Sometimes I do.

I'm a mom. I know I don't do everything right, but I also know I take care of my children. I hug them, snuggle them, discipline them, clothe them, feed them, play with them, teach them, laugh with them, and most of all, I love them fiercely.

That's what I know to be true.

So I think Mayor Mommy Guilt best be working on her résumé, because as far as I'm concerned, her term as Mayor of Guilt Town is up.

*   *   *

Another problem I have with Guilt is that she does not seem to be an equal opportunity offender. Everyone has felt guilt over something in his or her lifetime, but there are some people who would say for them, it's a rare occurrence. Those of us with guilt frequent flier miles can find this hard to understand.

I hate spiders. My aunt also hates spiders, and was telling me that when she finds one in her house, particularly the big juicy ones that seem to appear in the early fall, she has a pretty good routine for killing them. She hits them with a fly swatter, then picks them up with multiple paper towels and further squishes the corpse. Then she puts the body in the sink and washes it down the drain, and then she turns on the garbage disposal to finish the job.

I thought this was a good start. You cannot take spider killing too seriously. If there's an opportunity to use flame at some point in the death process, I'm good with that. Poison is a fine option too. This is not a time for weakness or partial effort.

With this understanding of my disdain for arachnids, you can see why during dinner, when I saw a medium-sized spider (smaller than a tarantula, bigger than the itsy-bitsy), crawling up the wall I gave quick orders for it to be executed.

"Karson, go kill that spider, quick! Hurry!"

Karson turned and looked at it and then back at me. "Hurry!" I repeated.

He got up and pulled three tissues out of the nearby box. He then reached high and pinched the spider in the tissues in his hand. On his way to the trash can, as he passed by the kitchen table where I still sat, he thought he'd be a wise-guy and act like he was going to throw the spider at me.

But he was not, in fact, a wise guy at that moment because an actual wise guy would have known not to even pretend to joke about this with me. Because when Karson made the throwing motion with his hand, the spider dislodged from the tissues, flew through the air, and hit me on the lip.

Sorry, I just blacked out there for a second. What was I saying?

Oh, yes, the moment of trauma.

I repeat, the spider hit me on the lip. As in, *I touched a spider with my mouth.*

I've heard of adrenaline surges that allow parents to pick up cars off their children who are trapped beneath. I had such a surge. I stood up so fast and began to chase my middle school son through the house with such a speed that it surprised us all. All I could think was, "Beat him up!"

"Beat him up!" Granted, he's a six-foot tall fourteen-year-old with arms that stretch like pulled taffy. I could probably not, under normal circumstances, actually beat him up. But these were not normal circumstances.

I just couldn't catch him.

He was laughing and my husband and daughters were vacillating between wanting to laugh, and being afraid to look me in the eye.

I spit, and stammered, and paced, and whined. It took me awhile to process the event both intellectually and emotionally. I kept wringing my hands and moaning.

"Mom, you're making this a big deal. It's not a big deal." Karson said while still trying to avoid my glare.

"Karson. A spider touched my mouth. There is no world in which that is not a big deal."

Later, Karson went on to tell me he really did not mean to throw the spider at all, that it surprised even him that it actually came out of the tissues. But nonetheless, he did not feel guilty about it.

And that is where I am going with this, folks. I am reliving my horror to tell you that not everyone feels guilt over the same things that would cause me tremendous, torturous guilt.

Some people are wired to let guilt bounce off of them like a spider off a lip. If you are one of those people, congratulations to you. Remember to tread lightly around those of us who may be more sensitive. If we confess we feel guilty about hurting you in some form or fashion, tell us you forgive us and remind us to let it go. Just because you don't feel the guilt in the same way we do doesn't mean it's not causing a strain on our shoulders and back muscles. Your acknowledgement, listening ear, and pardon can help lighten our load tremendously.

We all have our weaknesses. We all have those areas in life where we struggle and fret. For my son, that area should be in nervous waiting for me to enact my revenge.

He has been advised to sleep with one eye open.

*   *   *

Belated Birthday Treats

Originally posted on *Ten Blue Eyes* blog, September 28, 2012

I completely forgot.

My son and I have been discussing sending treats into school for his birthday for several weeks now. Karson even asked me to scope out some particular cookies while at the grocery store last week. We had a plan. He was looking forward to it. Today is the day.

I completely forgot.

I have not always been one to completely forget about something. When I was in high school I had a system that helped me remember things. If I were laying in bed, and suddenly remembered that I needed to take something to school the next morning or do something that next day, I would simply move my clock on my nightstand into a different position. I would turn it thirty degrees and that shift would trigger my memory the next day. True story. It seems ludicrous to me now! I'm almost incredulous at myself.

At this point in my life, if I were to unplug my clock, drag it downstairs by the cord and put it in the refrigerator I'm not confident that it would trigger anything in my memory the following day.

Thus, nothing helped me realize that today was the day to send the cookies.

It wasn't until I watched Karson wave to me from the bus window as it pulled away from the curb that I realized something wasn't right. Was I forgetting something? Wait! Where is my clock?

I gasped as it suddenly dawned on me that I hadn't sent the aforementioned cookies with Karson. In fact, I hadn't even purchased the aforementioned cookies! I slapped my hand on my forehead while my daughters looked at me and wondered what was wrong. "Get in the car, girls!" I stammered. "We've gotta go buy Karson's birthday treats and take them to his school!" Thankfully, they cooperated as briskly as two preschoolers can and like a sprinting turtle we were on our way.

Now, back to the cookies. The store didn't have any.

Strike two for Ol' Mommy. Now what?

I went over to the bakery counter and saw some cupcakes that had cute little footballs stuck in them. *Perfect. Karson is obsessed with football right now. These will be great.* But there weren't enough cupcakes for his entire class. All right. This was just a curve ball, not a strike. I asked the woman behind the counter if she had any more footballs I could put on some different cupcakes. She looked. They didn't.

Okay then. How about anything related to football, like a helmet or an Indianapolis Colts logo? Karson loves the Colts. She brought me some cute little helmets with the New England Patriots logo on them and asked if they were generic enough. "Uhhh ... no. That would be another team," I said. "I'm looking for the Colts with the little horseshoe."

Thankfully the other lady behind the counter knew a tad more about football (which isn't saying much) and found some Colts helmets. Touchdown!

The girls and I scurried into Karson's school with the cute football themed cupcakes. We did our due duties of signing in at the front office and then marched down the hall to deliver the goods. The teacher was standing in front of the board and was in the middle of teaching the class. I hesitantly peeked my head in the door. She motioned for me to set the treats on the counter in the back.

It was then that Karson saw us. His face lit up with a huge smile. He got up from his chair, came to me and gave me a big hug and a kiss on the cheek. Then he walked over to both of his sisters and kissed them as well. I almost cried. That boy just melts me. He is just who he is all the time. He had no inhibition about kissing me or his little sisters in front of the entire class. He simply loves others and expresses his love without any worry of what someone else may think. I adore this quality in both my son and my husband. They are so real and true to themselves in every setting. I want to be more like them.

Alright. Enough of the gush and mush. I need to get back to my to-do list. And come to think of it, I would like to add one more thing to remember to do.

#53: Forget to send Karson's birthday treats next year too.

Guilt and Regret are frequent opponents of mine. I've tried to call off the fight, but it's no use. I can't forever quiet the annoying taunts. There will always be a birthday-treat forgetting, spelling-test groaning, losing-my-cool moments that Guilt or Regret will try to exploit. But, with the help of Grace and Forgiveness, I put up a good fight. We're pretty scrappy teammates.

*   *   *

Slice of Hope: Grace and forgiveness can defeat guilt and regret. We need to accept them into our struggle, and then allow them to succeed.

IF ONLY IT WERE A PIECE OF CAKE

three

discontentment and insecurity

I sat across from her at the restaurant's colorful table. We both munched on our chips and salsa while we chatted. It had been awhile since we'd been able to catch up on each other's lives. It was refreshing to hear, and to be heard. But then the chatting turned into a real conversation. My sweet friend went a little deeper. She pushed open the door of her heart and allowed me to see inside where everything was not so neat and tidy. I saw wounds; some scarred over, and some that looked quite fresh. And she spoke of one aloud.

"I just don't feel content with my life."

I nodded.

"I don't really even understand why. I have everything I wanted and hoped for, but now I'm unhappy and discontented."

I nodded again. I was not only listening, I was hearing her with my heart. Because I understood. I have been there. Felt that way. Deeply. I recognized the aching wound.

Discontentment can sneak up on us and begin to wrap its cold hands around our hearts. The squeeze is slow, and not completely debilitating. But it's dangerous. Discontentment's gradual tightening tricks us into not really noticing it until we're suffering from it. At that point, its grip is locked in tight like a vise.

Discontentment can stem from a variety of roots. In my own life, it tends to surface after a storm, much like trash that is washed up onto a beach and left in the wake of a hurricane. It's ugly. It does nothing to help my current circumstances, and it needs attention.

In 2011, some discontentment trash washed up on my personal landscape. In the previous three years, I had weathered a mighty storm. As I've mentioned before, in 2007, our son, Karson, was diagnosed with leukemia. His chemotherapy and other treatments lasted more than three years and were finished in April of 2010. During those three years, I'd also given birth to two babies, and spent more hours in a hospital, for Karson's appointments, my own appointments, the babies' checkups, etc., than I can count. We were living in survival mode.

Many families with young children live in survival mode, whether or not they're dealing with a medical crisis. Everyday life with little ones can feel like a series of mini crises. This pulls your focus off thriving and teaching, and on to doing the necessary tasks of the day. The feeding, and the changing, and the rocking, and the feeding again, and making it to the child's bedtime, so Mom and Dad can sit down and have an uninterrupted conversation or moment alone. It's filling your coffee mug to the brim once again because your eyelids are drooping, and so are your spirits, because you only got two hours of sleep the night before when the newborn was fussy and the toddler had a bad dream.

For me, survival mode took on an entirely new meaning during that season. When you're helping your little boy fight for his very life with chemotherapy and spinal taps and steroids, survival mode becomes a literal lifestyle.

As with a torrential downpour, the rain does not usually stop in an instant. It gradually slows and suddenly it dawns on you that it's not raining anymore. You may stick your hand out from under the umbrella, or watch the puddles on the pavement for ripples, and you notice that they are still. The storm is over. Perhaps the sun is peeking through the clouds.

In 2011, when I came to realize the puddles in my life had stilled, and the worst of the survival mode was over, I was hesitant to accept it. Could it be that we were done with most of the hospital visits? Did I really sleep a solid eight hours last night? Are my baby and toddler daughters learning to laugh, and share, and eat solid foods, and self-soothe during naptime? Were the oral chemotherapy bottles gone from my countertops? Was my calendar filling with playdates instead of procedures, outings instead of oncologist appointments? I'd stick my hand out from under my umbrella and wait. Nothing. My hand was dry. Perhaps the storm had ended, after all.

That's when I began to notice the trash littered on the shoreline, for winds and storms bring things buried deep to the surface. The survival mindset gave way to confusion and uncertainty. In a sense, I was now drifting instead of driven. The effects of the storm had taken a toll on my own body and mind. I felt weathered. I got sick. The combination of reemerging into society after three years of isolation (due to Karson's weakened immune system), and the fading adrenaline and urgency assaulted me. I gained weight. I seemed to catch every stomach bug and cold that was "going around." Aimlessness and discontentment descended on me.

But why?

I shared my feelings one day with a mentor and friend of mine, Terri. Terri is one of those people whose comments and quotes should be made into magnets and greeting cards. She says wise and profound things in our conversations.

"When Karson was sick," Terri said, "you certainly did not have to wonder what your purpose was, did you?" She continued, "As difficult as it was, there was no question. You knew what you had to do as his mother and as the mother of your girls. That clarity can actually be a blessing. When you don't have it anymore, it can be a struggle."

Terri was saying that my purpose during the years of 2007-2010 possessed laser focus. Though not the purpose I chose for myself, nor would I ever choose it again, it was clear. Take care of Karson. Help him fight for his life. Carry healthy pregnancies, give birth, and take care of Karly and Kenzie. Fight for love in my marriage to Kraig in the midst of the chaos. Head down. Full steam ahead.

Now, the crystal-clear purpose for my life had vanished.

And discontentment washed ashore.

Because when we don't know or feel our purpose, it's hard to know if we're achieving it. We feel aimless, and maybe useless.

Even though I was still caring for three children and nourishing my marriage and friendships, none of them seemed as urgent or as vital as they had in the previous years.

Now I began to question my purpose, and in turn, my day-to-day tasks. Was I still doing this parenting thing correctly? Is that what the preschool years are supposed to look like? Is my marriage growing and healthy in this normal, mundane stuff of life? What should my friendships look like now that they are less focused on our children?

"Take son to chemotherapy appointment so that he can receive the drugs necessary to kill his cancer" seems so much worthier and more critical than, "Take son to basketball practice so he can learn how to shoot a free throw." Therein lies the problem with purpose. We think that if we aren't doing something "worthy" or "critical," then it must not be our purpose. We wonder if the everyday things of life should be worthy of our devotion. How can dish washing, diaper changing, homework helping, trash emptying, gas pumping, check cashing, spreadsheet writing, phone answering, good-night story reading moments be meaningful?

But they are.

I needed to believe this for myself in post-storm 2011. I needed to give the discontentment trash that had littered my shoreline some of my attention. I had to clean up the damage the storm had done.

Changing my mindset proved to be the key. I worked to relearn and remind myself that the ordinary is not lesser than the extraordinary.

The ordinary is not lesser than the extraordinary. In fact, without the ordinary, there would be no extraordinary.

As I've been involved in various Bible studies and small groups where we've had great group discussions, I've noticed a common thread. Often, a disconnect exists between what we learn and study, and what we actually apply to our actual lives. We as humans sometimes have a short circuit in the wiring between our ears and our feet. We may hear it, but we don't move on it.

Maybe it's because we feel like we can't relate to the "bigness" we're learning about from the Bible story. We read about a man who leads millions of Israelites out of Egypt and, by God's mighty hand, parts the Red Sea. Then they walk across on dry land. I've never experienced such a thing.

As I taught this story to a group of high school girls, one of them asked me if a dolphin could have jumped from one wall of water, over the people, to the other side. I laughed as I pictured it for myself.

"I don't know!" I said. "I wasn't there. I've never seen the walls of water for myself or felt the dry land under my feet."

Then we have Joshua and his people who walk around a city for seven days. Sure, the people of Jericho thought they were nuts, but they ate their words (and their dust?) a week later when the walls of their city fell.

People literally walking in obedience around walls. Walls literally falling down. I've not experienced this sort of thing. I've been around things that fall down. Snow forts, toy block towers, kids who spun themselves silly in Ring-Around-The-Rosie, but never city walls. What I've seen with my own eyes doesn't seem as big.

Then we have the New Testament. Oh, my goodness! Peter walking on water, water being turned into wine, leprosy turning into smooth healthy skin, and people literally coming back from the dead.

This is big stuff.

We read about it and we think, "This is not what my life looks like. No walls are falling down when I blow my trumpet and scream. My feet not only get wet when I jump into water, but I'm in up to my eyeballs! I know people who are sick and are not being healed. And I've never witnessed anyone come back from the dead.

How am I supposed to relate to this big stuff? How can I apply these Bible stories to my own life? How am I to feel as if I have purpose in my own life when what I do is so dull in comparison?

I get it. But one thing I have to remember is that the people we read about in the Bible had dull days too. Sure, the folks who marched around Jericho and saw the walls fall had something to write home about that week. They'd also recently seen the Jordan River part as they began this campaign into the Promised Land. But, what about the days and weeks and months before they received their marching orders? We know nothing very extraordinary about their lives and the days before the Jordan parting and Jericho falling "biggies."

Yes, they had the daily miracle of manna and quail. But they didn't see it as the miracle it was. They saw it as an everyday occurrence—kind of dull after awhile. I think we see Pop-Tarts, and cheeseburgers, and lattes much the same way. We don't realize what an extraordinary thing they are!

Yes, we read about Joshua, the leader of the Israelites, doing some amazing things during the pre-Promised Land days, but what about the hundreds of other folks? Their lives were so ordinary before the walls fell, we know nothing of them individually. They were hanging out in the wilderness. Chillin'. Or whatever it's called when you live in the desert.

Guess what? Most of the time, the majority of us are just living our lives in the wilderness, waiting for God to allow us to enter the Promised Land too. The Jordan and Jericho days are the exception, not the rule.

I look at Ruth of the Bible too. She encountered a tough set of circumstances in an otherwise seemingly normal life that led to her being someone we read about today. Let me explain.

Ruth lived in a place called Moab. Her husband died. We don't know how or why, but we know she and her sister-in-law, Orpah, who had married her husband's brother, are now both widows. So is their mother-in-law, Naomi. Naomi is a native Israelite, but the daughters-in-law are both from Moab.

Naomi decides to return to Israel and the girls begin the journey with her, but she encourages them to go back home to Moab and start new lives. Orpah eventually agrees to return home, but Ruth does not. She remains faithful and loyal to Naomi, and more importantly, she vows to take Naomi's God and be loyal to Him.

When they reach Israel, Bethlehem specifically, they are two women living alone without a means of income. Naomi comes up with a plan and advises Ruth to gather leftover wheat from fields of one of their distant relatives, Boaz.

Ruth works in the field. Boaz notices her. Eventually he takes her to be his wife and they have a son together whose name is Obed. Obed becomes the father of Jesse, and Jesse has a son named David. King David. The one we talked about earlier who was kind to his best friend's crippled son. This is also the same guy who fought Goliath, played the harp, had an affair, and repented of his sin, and is remembered to this day as one of Israel's greatest kings.

Ruth was his great-grandma! Ruth, the Moab woman who had a seemingly ordinary life and, for most of her days, just did normal things. She got married, she was widowed, she got remarried, she had a child, she raised the child, she took care of her mother-in-law.

She also spent some of her days not knowing where her next paycheck was going to come from while she and Naomi were widowed and alone. She spent days in the hot middle-eastern sun picking up sheaves of grain. She didn't know in those moments, as sweat rolled down her back, and her calf muscles ached from walking in the hard soil, that she would one day be grafted in to the line of Christ. As in, most literally put into his family lineage. She didn't know when she was choosing to care for her lonely mother-in-law, and leave her own familiar country to travel with her, that she'd meet another man who would love her and take her to be his wife. She didn't know while she did housework and had plain run-of-the-mill conversations with the ladies in the market that one day she'd be remembered as the king's great-grandmother.

Not all of her days were extraordinary, but we remember her that way.

Not all of your days will be extraordinary either. In fact, most of them will not. Most will be spent repeating tasks you've done more times than you can count. Making small talk in the checkout lane at the grocery store, or picking your child up from school and taking her to a dental appointment. Nothing that seemingly shows purpose or destiny.

But the ordinary days of picking wheat led to Ruth being in the line of David, and ultimately, Jesus, the Bread of Life!

I don't know the end of my story, or what I'll be remembered for. But I don't have to know the ending to live the now. Even though I can't see the purpose or the reason or the extraordinary, doesn't mean I'm not where God wants me to be. God seems to call people into extraordinary moments from ordinary work. Ruth gleaned in the field. David tended his sheep. Peter fished on his boat. They all were getting the work done in the most ordinary ways, and doing the work in front of them without knowing the end result. When God led them to opportunities or called them to Himself, they obeyed.

And God took it from there.

My favorite biblical example of ordinary people, in an ordinary place, who experienced an extraordinary moment? The shepherds to whom the angels told of Jesus' birth. Talk about people just doing their job and getting on with life. These guys probably hadn't had an extraordinary existence until that evening. The fact that they were shepherds in a fairly small town proves their ordinariness. Not kings. Not movie stars. Not even lawyers or biology teachers. They took care of sheep for a living. Sheep. Maybe throw in some camels and goats, but still, they ranked pretty low on the prestige scale. They saw the same scenery each day and night. They were probably buddies, sitting around a fire most evenings, talking about nothing spectacular. Ordinary.

And then one evening everything changed.

An angel of the Lord appeared to them and said, "Do not be afraid." That he says this indicates they probably were a little freaked out. Who wouldn't be? An angel shows up out of nowhere and tells them "good news that would bring great joy for all people." (Luke 2) The news that the Messiah had been born in their town. The One that would rule forever and bring peace and hope to all men was born in their town!

This is the best news they, or any of us for that matter, could have heard. This is life changing. This is world changing. This is eternity changing. The shepherds, just normal guys out with their sheep, heard the news first. And then they were given the opportunity to go *see* Jesus. They were among the very first to meet him personally.

Suddenly, their ordinary lives became extraordinary.

But notice this. They didn't orchestrate it. They didn't plan it. They really had nothing to do with it. They didn't brainstorm or vision-cast, "Hey guys, let's be the first to hear about the Messiah's birth. Meet me in the field Christmas day. Wear your ugly sweaters."

No! Of course not! They had nothing to do with the extraordinary. They just were doing their ordinary jobs, on an ordinary night, when God broke through the mundane and changed their worlds.

This makes me feel good. I can relate to the shepherds. I've never spent much face-to-face time with a sheep, but I've been known to live in some pretty ordinary moments. To know that living in the ordinary is all that is really required of me in order for God to show up and do the extraordinary, well that makes me smile.

In 2011, my purpose seemed too ordinary, and in turn, that translated to me thinking my purpose wasn't good or big enough. I was just doing normal housework, and mom work, and life tasks. My friend, Terri, was right. Not having a laser-focused purpose led to a struggle. Feeling like my purpose was not good enough led to discontentment.

Discontentment is a thief. It robs us of joy, and of living in the moment we've been given. It's an ugly thing. Trash on the shore, and all of that.

I've been there. I had to do some cleanup work on my shores. It took effort and a decision to obey in the ordinary, and to find it to be extraordinary in and of itself. But it was worth it.

I'll probably be there in the struggle again someday. In fact, I think I can remove the word "probably" from that last sentence. I think it's a guarantee. In those moments of struggle, I want to remember to be faithful with what is in front of me. To do the work. To love God, and to love others loyally. To take care of my sheep. To show up in the field. To see and accept the opportunities God provides. When He calls and leads, to obey.

And to let God take it from there.

*   *   *

Finding Sense in the Common

Originally posted on *Ten Blue Eyes* blog, November 11, 2016

I pull the spoon out of the dishwasher and stack it with its fellow tablemates in the drawer. My motions are robotic. I do this same thing almost every single day. It is such a common task that I don't even have to concentrate on what I am doing.

I push the clothes into the drum of the washing machine and reach up to grab the detergent. My mind is thinking about something else. There is no need to pay attention to each motion of the laundry routine. It is a common work in my life, and I have memorized the actions it takes to complete it.

"Grab your book bag."

"Where are your shoes?"

"You will need a jacket today."

All common phrases heard in my home each weekday morning. The same idea. The same routine. Over and over. And then almost always, I see the same results.

My life feels so common.

Being common doesn't feel very empowering. It's just so plain and normal. So mundane and run-of-the-mill. So regular. Isn't that basically the definition of the word itself?

Common.

How can being common be significant?

How can my common life make a difference in this world? How can God use my common routine for His glory? How can common amount to anything at all?

But surely it does.

It just sometimes hides behind the extraordinary.

In the Old Testament, in the book of Genesis, Joseph does an amazing work of interpreting Pharaoh's dreams in regards to a coming famine. He leads the Egyptians in the storing of food for seven years in order to survive the impending drought. His ability and his leadership is so uncommon. He saves a nation from starvation.

But behind his uncommonness are the common. The farmers. The men and women who each day do the work of planting, and tending, and harvesting. The people who put their hands to the plow. The people whose run-of-the-mill tasks grew the very food that was stored and that saved.

The common work provided daily bread for the saving of many lives.

Solomon, in his riches and splendor, in his uncommon life as a King of Israel, built a temple in Jerusalem that stunned the onlooker. It was majestic and extraordinary. But behind the amazing structure hid the men who cut the stones in the quarry. Who day-in and day-out did the heavy lifting. Whose brows dripped with sweat and whose muscles grew strong. They did the common daily difficult labor.

The common work laid the very foundation for the House of God.

A crowd of 5,000 hungry men sat waiting to hear Jesus. They then witnessed a wondrous moment when the lunch of a small boy fed them all. Their stomachs were full because of an uncommon miracle of God. Yet, behind the miracle, there was probably a mama who had simply packed her son's lunch. She did the mundane, common task that she probably had done hundreds of times before. She did not know that the very hands of God would take the fruits of the labor, as meager as they were, and multiply them for the glory of God the Father.

The common work fed a multitude and pointed many to the power of God.

So my hands will continue to do the common work. To unload the dishes and reload the washing machine. To pack the book bags and tend to the growth of the children. To complete the tasks that seem insignificant.

Because in the hands of God, the common is extraordinary, after all.

*   *   *

I scroll through social media and find myself pausing over certain photos. Sometimes I zoom in and study further. Hair curled in perfect waves. Straight white teeth. A slim waistline and skinny legs. Cute clothes. I'm taking inventory. I'm noticing all of the ways this woman is beautiful. But I'm not forming a well-crafted compliment to leave in the comments. My critique is part of my comparison habit. I'm comparing her to me.

Comparison leads to discontentment and insecurity. Hardly an earth shattering statement. In fact, I can hear you thinking, "Tell me something I don't know, girl."

Comparison is a big bully. She's grabbed me by the hair many times and has dragged me down to the ground. It's embarrassing to admit. But, I've had many friends (both social media ones and actual warm-to-the-touch ones) who have admitted they've had some go-rounds with Comparison too. She's a busy bully.

Comparison has attacked me from two different directions.

For one, we all know (if you're an actual warm-to-the-touch human) that we can feel discontent and insecure by comparing our "goods" to others. I'm referring to the actual good things in our lives.

We compare our physical physiques and clothing. We compare our homes, décor, children, children's behavior, husbands, husbands' behavior, jobs, talents, personalities, likes and dislikes, friendships, and the list goes on and on.

It's not fun. Because no matter how much you like your goods, you might like one piece of someone else's better. And so forth. Just as there's always something to be thankful for, there's always something to feel bad about. Comparison magnifies those things about which we like to feel bad.

I've heard other writers and speakers use the phrase "stay in your lane," when it comes to our own personalities, talents, etc. I like it. I can think of very practical reasons and examples where staying in your own lane is a good thing.

Driving. Can you imagine someone who drives with two wheels in each lane on the highway for miles (Road Rage, anyone?)? What about swimming laps? My husband was faithfully exercising this way, and came home to tell me one evening that he'd miscommunicated with a fellow swimmer. They'd collided head first (going opposite directions in the same lane) and he'd given the guy a nose bleed in the pool. Oops.

For me, my youngest child is constantly walking in my lane. Literally. She's eight years old, and while walking beside me, somehow always drifts in front of my feet and ends up nearly tripping me. I tell her to stay in her lane and get out of my way. Sometimes I say it nicer than that. A few minutes later, she's almost walking on my toes again.

Comparison is another great reason for staying in your lane. We all have our own life lanes. We're not meant to do and have it all. We're meant to do what we're meant to do, and have what we have. By doing so, we can help each other!

Not long ago, I walked into a local coffee shop to grab a cup of joe to go. But, before I could get to the counter to order, I walked by a table where two of my friends sat. They were working on taxes and financial reports for the business one of them owns. The financial business owner of the two asked me if I was writing another book. I told her I was, in fact, working on one (the one you're holding now!) and I told her I had written about 42,000 words thus far.

"Oh! I just threw up in my mouth a little when you said that!" she said dryly.

I laughed and said, "Well, what you're doing right now with numbers and math looks terrible to me!"

We're both serving a purpose right now with our talents. And we both greatly admire and appreciate what the other one does! I believe it's part of God's current purpose for each of us. We know our lanes. We're staying in them. It's a good thing.

So comparison can come at us from the direction of comparing our "goods" with others. A good way to combat her from that angle is to stay in your own lane and be who God made you to be.

.*   *   *

The Masterpiece

Originally posted on *Ten Blue Eyes* blog, March 11, 2014

The cry derailed my train of thought and interrupted my task of emptying the dishwasher. I looked up and watched as my two daughters, who were painting with watercolors at the kitchen table, dramatically expressed their feelings. My five-year-old daughter had tears streaming down her face and her three-year-old sister was crying as well, with her little arms crossed in stubborn indignation.

I sighed and rested my hands on the countertop where the bowls and plates waited to be put back into the cupboard so that they could rest in peace. I was wishing for peace as well. Playing referee to these two could be draining.

When the crying didn't stop, I sent the youngest, who seemed to be the cause of the problem, up to her room and I followed a few minutes later to have "a talk."

"What's the deal, Kenzie?" I asked her as she wiped her tears while sitting on her bed. "Why are you so upset and frustrated with your sister?"

She drew her breath in quickly several times while trying to speak. Finally she said, "But Mama! Karly said she was painting a boat but I don't think it looks like a boat at all. I think she's painting a rocket ship!"

I had to do the old "parent trick" of looking sideways and pretending I suddenly had to scratch my cheek so that I could cover the smile that spread across my face. What could I say? It did look an awfully lot like a rocket.

But Karly had said that she painted a boat and who was I to disagree?

So I gently explained to little sis that even though she was right in thinking that it did look like a rocket, it also looked like a boat too.

It was Karly's workmanship, created to be a boat no matter what the rest of us thought it should be.

The paints have long been cleaned up and the dishes have been through the wash cycle and back into the cupboard countless times since that moment. But I've continued to chuckle to myself about Kenzie's honest assessment of Karly's painting.

That moment has made me think about something more.

I've thought about the fact that I am a masterpiece too. I was created and I am supposed to be something specific. Not a boat or a rocket ship … but me. I am God's masterpiece, and no matter what anyone else thinks I should look like or should be, I am His creation.

Ephesians 2:10 says, "For we are God's handiwork, created in Christ Jesus to do good works, which God prepared in advance for us to do."

The word "handiwork" in this verse is the original Greek word "poiema" which, according to Strong's Concordance means, "that which has been made; a work: of the works of God as creator."

I'm God's masterpiece. I am called to be who He created me to be.

Sometimes I worry about being what others think I should be. Am I still valuable if I'm "just me?"

I have friends who juggle both careers and motherhood and they don't drop the ball in either role. I don't work outside the home. Does that make me less valuable than they?

I know children who are amazing and committed athletes *and* musicians. My kids have never had a single piano lesson. I'm not the mother of a prodigy. Am I less significant than those who are?

I have a college degree, but much like my computer, which falls asleep when it's not touched for awhile, my skills and practical application of my schooling feel like they're dormant and hiding. Does this mean I'm unsuccessful?

So once again I go back to Ephesians 2:10. I was, "created in Christ Jesus to do good works, which God prepared in advance."

God has prepared works for me in advance so that all I have to do is be *me* and be obedient to *Him.* If I'm made in Christ Jesus then I certainly have been equipped to accomplish what He calls me to do because Jesus is full of power and never-ending grace.

I don't have to force myself to be a rocket ship if God created me to be a boat. I can just be me because that is who God made me to be. I am significant and beautiful in His eyes. He will go with me and help me to accomplish what He has prepared for me to do. It's extra beautiful because it's all for His glory.

No matter what others see, my Creator knows just who I am.

And I am His masterpiece.

*   *   *

Comparison can also attack from the other side. She can hurt you by not only in comparing your "goods" with others, but also in comparing your "bads."

In this attack angle, we feel guilt for not having a big enough "bad," compared to another, to warrant our struggle. Perhaps we think that if our struggle isn't "bad enough" then we shouldn't be having such a hard time dealing with it. Why can't we just do better? Why am I struggling with something that is minor compared with what she's dealing with over there? I'm such a loser. I can't even deal with my "bads" the correct way.

I have been on both sides of this. I've whined about a small "bad" in my life, and then my friend, with whom I'm having lunch, and who has fought cancer for more than a decade, updates me on her current circumstances. I've walked away from these lunches reeling, my perspective shaken. I just want to kick myself for being such a big baby and whining about something that's minuscule in comparison to what my friend is facing.

On the flip side, years ago, I was in the midst of a "big bad" in my own life, when my son was undergoing his chemotherapy treatments.

I was taking a walk with three girlfriends, and we were discussing our days. They each took a turn sharing something that had happened that day. One of them was dealing with an impending move across the county and was telling us about the showings and the daunting to-do list ahead. The other two friends each shared something frustrating they'd dealt with that day, and then they turned to me.

I had been quiet. I knew that I held the "bad day" trump card. I knew that by telling them that we'd been at the children's hospital two hours away from home that day (and therefore had driven four hours) and had spent several hours watching our very sick son get chemo, I was going to close the book on the conversation. I was going to be the victor of the bad day game, and I didn't want to be. I didn't want to say anything. I remember so clearly knowing that the day I'd had had been rotten, but also knowing that my friends had truly struggled in their own days. I didn't want to invalidate their own struggles. Because they *were* valid. Even when our struggles or feelings are small in comparison to someone else's, it doesn't mean they are not still legitimate.

I always try to support my beliefs with the Bible. Remarkably, the Bible always comes through. I believe it's because the Bible is God's Word, and as Hebrews 4:12 says, it is "living and active." It doesn't grow stale or have an expiration date.

So, I look to Scripture and I see that Jesus himself modeled the idea of validating the struggles of others even when they could be seen as "small bads." Let's face it, Jesus could have always played his cards differently. He held the trump card of "bads." He lived a perfect life, and then died for the sins of mankind. No one else in the history of the world has held that card. Or will anyone, ever.

Yet, Jesus was compassionate. He didn't compare his struggles with the struggles of others, and, he didn't seem to compare one man's struggle with another man's. He just loved each one where they were. He validated their pain and feelings. Don't believe me? Look up these examples for yourself.

Jesus healed many. He healed people from a variety of issues. Some of those issues or diseases could have been viewed as "bigger bads" than others. He healed a fever (Matthew 8:14) which maybe seems less bad than leprosy (Matthew 8:3).

He cast out demons (Matthew 8:16) which may seem like a "bigger bad" than general illness (Matthew 8:16).

He healed a dear bleeding woman who humbly touched Jesus' cloak in order to receive His power while He's on his way to raise a child from the dead. (Matthew 9:20-26) He didn't tell the bleeding woman that her problem was lesser, that a child was dead, and her bleeding was nothing in comparison. He met each person where they were in their "bad." He loved them and cared for them and validated their pain and hurts.

He healed blind people, mute people, lame people. He didn't ever rank ailments.

He fed hungry crowds. He didn't tell them their empty stomachs weren't worthy of his miraculous power.

He told an entire parable (Matthew 18:10-14) about losing one sheep and how even though ninety-nine were still safe in the flock, He went after the one. Some of us would put the needs of the majority over those of the few. This one sheep might have had it coming, anyway. But Jesus cared for each individual. Those lost, and those found.

The night before his excruciating death, Jesus could have completely focused on his own sorrow. Instead, He focused on those whom He loved. His apostles. He washed their stinky, dirty feet. (John 13:1-5) He served them knowing they too would suffer in the coming days, weeks, and months. He supplied the first communion, the beautiful symbolism he presented with the bread and cup. He knew and cared about their anxieties. Maybe most of all, He saw them. Each one. As individuals, and as friends whom He loved. He saw their hurts, their futures, their hearts, and their hopes.

Jesus didn't compare the disciples to one another. He didn't allow Peter's denial or John's charming personality to lose them points or gain them merit. He drew them each to a relationship with Himself. He wanted them to find security in His presence—just as they were. No matter their failures or ugliness.

He saw them. And He loved them.

And He sees me too.

*　　*　　*

The Visible Woman

Originally posted on my church's women's ministry blog, February 12, 2013

Her real name is Susan Storm Richards, but most know her better by her alias: The Invisible Woman.

According to *Marvel's* website, this member of the Fantastic Four has powers that allow her to "render herself wholly or partially invisible at will."

This could be handy. I'd enjoy being invisible at times. It would be interesting to hear what others say about me when I walk out of a room and perhaps more fun to wreak havoc on friends and family members by appearing at will when they least expect me!

But if I'm being honest, I don't really wish to be invisible. In fact, being invisible can be a disadvantage.

As a woman, wife, mother, and human I can attest that there are times that I feel invisible … but it doesn't strike me as a super power.

Instead, it stings as a frustration.

When my perspective vanishes and I allow my attitude to get out of line, I feel like I'm the Invisible Woman. I work hard all day and yet it's not noticed or recognized by anyone. The tasks I do need to be repeated again and again and my wheels spin in a thankless, exhausting rut. No one sees what I'm doing or cares … unless I fail to accomplish what they want, and then suddenly I'm seen, but only as a failure.

Am I really invisible? Does no one care? Can anyone take the time to stop for a moment to see me and meet my needs, for once?

I've lost sight of the truth about God's love.

I think a servant girl from the Old Testament can relate. In fact, she was the original Invisible Woman, although Marvel doesn't acknowledge her on their website.

Hagar was the maidservant of Sarai. Sarai was the barren wife of Abram who so desperately wanted a child she gave her maidservant to her husband hoping to produce a child through their union. Hagar was a means to an end. She was used only for what she could produce. Once Hagar did, in fact, get pregnant with Abraham's child, she despised her mistress. The feeling was mutual. Sarai loathed Hagar.

"Then Sarai mistreated Hagar; so [Hagar] fled from her. The angel of the Lord found Hagar near a spring in the desert; it was the spring that is beside the road to Shur. And he said, 'Hagar, slave of Sarai, where have you come from, and where are you going?' 'I'm running away from my mistress Sarai,' she answered. Then the angel of the Lord told her, 'Go back to your mistress and submit to her.'" (Genesis 16:6-9)

The angel of Lord proceeded to give Hagar a prophecy about her unborn son. He spoke to this maidservant. He not only saw this seemingly invisible woman, He also knew her circumstances and spoke directly to her.

Hagar's response?

"She gave this name to the Lord who spoke to her: 'You are the God who sees me,' for she said, 'I have now seen the One who sees me.'" (Genesis 16:13)

For the first recorded time in the Old Testament, God is addressed as El Roi; "The God who sees me." Hagar finally knew someone cared for and saw her.

How great is God's love for each and every one. While we become consumed with our lives, our selves, and our tasks, we lose sight of the truth about God's powerful love.

But His love requires obedience on our end too. God told Hagar to go back to her mistress and submit to her. It may sound harsh, but by doing so God was giving her a way to be cared for and for his prophecy to be carried out to completion. I love how this command is worded in the Young's Literal Translation.

"'Turn back unto thy mistress, and humble thyself under her hands.'"

God offered Hagar His great mercy and love. She just had to humble herself to receive it.

Lamentations 3:22-23 says, "Because of the Lord's great love we are not consumed, for his compassions never fail. They are new every morning."

Because of the Lord's great love. Not because we've worked so hard. Not because we are superwomen. Not because of anything we have done. But because of the Lord's great love.

We don't have the super power. He does.

I'm not invisible. El Roi sees me. He knows me. He made me. He cares about me. He loves me.

I simply need to humble myself under His merciful and loving hands. By obeying God's Word and trusting in His never failing compassions I regain my focus on the Truth.

I become The Visible Woman, with the power "to render myself wholly valuable and unconditionally loved by the God who see me."

Take that, Susan Storm Richards!

*　　*　　*

My grandpa, whom I call Pappy, is one of the most humble and kind people I've ever met. He constantly is making us, his family, feel loved and accepted. We've teased him for years that every birthday card message he writes says the same thing: "I'm so proud of you!" We could be drug dealers living in the city landfill and Pappy would still find a way to express what great qualities we possess.

We'd also laugh after my middle school band concerts when Pappy would tell me, one of fourteen flutists, that he could hear my flute above everyone else, and I was the best. Yeah, right, Pappy. But his unconditional support and grandfatherly pride is endearing and gives me such security.

When I face Insecurity, I strive to redirect my focus. It helps to remember that, just like Pappy, God sees me and loves me for who I am. When I picture myself being seen by Him, it removes the pressure of being seen by other people. God loves me. Just as true, God *likes* me!

God created me to be me. Despite my broken parts, my bumps, rolls, and scars, He loves me. He loves me enough to redeem me from my sin and make a way for me to be with Him for eternity. (Romans 5:8, John 3:16) He doesn't do this because I'm perfect or worthy, but because He is. That truth helps me turn my insecurity into confidence.

Not a boastful conceit, but a confidence in who I am because of the promise of *Whose* I am.

I am secure in God's love. Sure, I'm not perfect. I'm a whiny mess of mistakes, and disappointments, and unfulfilled to-do lists. I may not be as pretty or smart as the next girl. I may have flaws and failures and brokenness inside that no one else even knows about.

But Insecurity can take a hike. Because my daddy, my Heavenly Father, loves me. And that is where I find my earthly confidence.

*　　*　　*

Slice of Hope: God sees you and loves you right where you are. Don't compare yourself to others! Stay in your lane while validating the successes and struggles of others. Loving God is obeying Him, even if the tasks seem lesser than another's, or too ordinary to matter. Obedience to God is extraordinary, after all.

IF ONLY IT WERE A PIECE OF CAKE

four
love and like

Love and Like. Ahh! A little respite from the difficulties of worry, anxiety, discontentment, insecurity, guilt, and regret. An indulgent chapter into which we can dive—something easy and sweet. A side of ice cream to go with that cake?

I'm sorry. No.

This is still a section about life's tough moments—the relational moments. Though the words "love and like" sound so cheery, we all know that real-life love and relationships are not always going to put a smile on our faces.

In fact, in my life, the people that I love and like the most are the ones who make me the most angry, annoyed, and crazy. That's because I know them. I interact with them, and they know and interact with me. We all have unique personalities, opinions, interests, even driving records, and we sometimes don't relate to someone else's. You already understand this, so why am I explaining it to you?

Kraig tells me I over-explain things all the time. He says I repeat my point in various ways and continue talking when he understood the point five sentences ago. Kraig tells me this because I know him and interact with him, and because he's my husband. And because sometimes he wants me to shut up.

We laugh about this.

Sometimes I continue explaining even after I know he understands. This makes us laugh harder. He tells me to shut up through his grin, and I keep going through my chuckle.

The challenging moments within Love and Like certainly are not limited to marriage. That being said, many of my most delightful moments, and my most deeply hurtful moments, have occurred in my marriage. Sometimes the love I feel for Kraig is almost palpable. It's warm and fuzzy and wonderful. Other times, the saying, "It's a good thing I love you, because I don't like you right now," rings more true.

I don't have this Love and Like thing figured out. I will not pretend to. But, I will tell you something that has helped me in the difficult moments of Love and Like.

Sweet mercy!

No, I've not transformed into an exclamatory southern belle. Mercy brings a sweet relief to the difficult moments of Love and Like.

Mercy has been defined by the Oxford dictionary as "compassion or forgiveness shown toward someone whom it is within one's power to punish or harm."

In other words, compassion or forgiveness shown toward anyone. Why anyone? Because we all have the power to punish or harm another human, whether it be by our words, actions, or sticks and stones.

Understand that mercy is undeserved. It's not earned. In Love and Like, we'd like it to be an equal give and take. A balanced vessel. Sometimes it is. But, in the difficult moments of hurt and pain from words or actions, we need to employ mercy to help right the ship.

Employing mercy looks like not giving someone the response you think they deserve. Not lashing out. Not repaying a wound with a wound. It looks like putting yourself in their shoes and acting on empathy instead of revenge.

Mercy can take many forms. Even that of a popcorn bowl.

*   *   *

The Popcorn Bowl

Originally posted on *Ten Blue Eyes* blog, April 14, 2012

What do I think of when I think of true love, commitment, and romance? You'll probably never guess. Okay, maybe if you read the title of this post you've got a good idea. Otherwise, would you believe our popcorn bowl is what triggers reminders for me of how much I love my husband?

Yeah, it sounds crazy. But I'm going to let you in on an intimate detail of our marriage. Here goes. My husband loves to eat popcorn in the evenings. When he's done with his snack, he leaves the popcorn bowl, full of kernels, on the counter. This irks me. Yep, that's the intimate detail.

This has been going on for years now. Can he just throw the kernels away and wash the crazy bowl by himself? Yes, he very well could. But he doesn't.

Now, we have a pretty traditional marriage where I do almost all of the cooking and cleaning. I'm good with this and enjoy it, for the most part. But the difference has been that I don't usually use the popcorn bowl myself as opposed to when I make dinner and use the dishes for all of our family. So, the popcorn bowl feels different. Like it's sitting there ... just one more thing I'm expected to do before I head to bed.

This has gotten me a little steamed ... and eventually my inner kernel popped! I finally voiced my displeasure one night, and asked why he expected this bowl to magically become clean and appear in the cupboard for his next salty rendezvous.

His response? He hadn't even thought about it. He wasn't intentionally leaving more work for me to do. To him it was like any other dish we used in our home.

Really?! Did he not realize I didn't use the bowl? That I felt used myself because he just expected me to put it away? This was news to him....

So how does this story end? Has something changed? Does Kraig now wash the bowl every time and return it to its rightful place in the cupboard? Yes, something has changed ... but it's not anything Kraig does.

What's changed? My perspective. When I realized he wasn't intentionally trying to get my proverbial goat, I decided to change how I viewed the popcorn bowl. Now I see it as a round, shiny, salty, and silly little labor of love. I know, it's weird. But, it's a regular reminder to me now of how much I love this man.

I know he could easily wash it himself, and he's even offered. But now for me it's a tangible way to remind *me* of how much I love him. I've realized this doesn't work if I do it with a bad attitude. But if I think of washing that bowl as a way to express how much I love Kraig, I even sometimes smile while scrubbing that thing clean.

We've got wedding rings and three kids to remind us of our commitment and history together. They are great reminders too. But on a regular basis, I've got a popcorn bowl to help me with this kernel of wisdom: *I love the man who eats the popcorn.* When I think of all he does for me and for our children, I can season the menial tasks of my day with a proper perspective. And, that has made the popcorn bowl a savory symbol of romance in my eyes.

Now, if I could only do the same with the clothes hamper.

*   *   *

If you think I'm all sweet and holy and that I employ mercy in this establishment full-time, you're wrong. When I wrote this blog about the popcorn bowl, I had worked through some anger, and bitterness, and resentment in that particular scenario, and I'd come to the conclusion that I can show mercy to Kraig by washing the bowl and remembering all the ways he cares for our family.

Sometimes I still do wash the bowl with a wonderful, merciful attitude.

But this is not a fairy tale, folks.

"Happily-ever-after" should be replaced with "sometimes I still get angry about the stupid popcorn bowl." It doesn't have the same ring to it, does it?

Maybe it's not the popcorn bowl, but the milk he's left out on the counter, or the shoes he's abandoned in the middle of the family room floor, or the clothes that I had folded now laying in a heap on the floor. Honestly, no matter the trigger, sometimes I just don't want to show mercy. *I just don't want to.*

Instead, I want him to show mercy to *me.*

It can be ugly. My heart can hold on to frustration that can lead to bitterness that can lead to unkind words and actions. I'm not talking about poisoning his piece of cake or anything, maybe just not making him one at all. And we're back to the difficult parts of Love and Like again. We never really left, did we? The difficult parts are intertwined within it all.

I find it very difficult to show mercy to someone if I feel they didn't earn it. Ironically, that's the whole point. They wouldn't need mercy if they deserved it.

However, I want things to be fair and even. Just and right. I'll be happy to show mercy to someone if I think they deserve it, but if they have mistreated me, even in the smallest manner, I get ugly inside. I guess if I'm being honest, it feels good to replay my "rightness" and their "wrongness." I feel somewhat vindicated.

It's sinful. That's what it really boils down to.

So often, when I feel wronged or angry at someone I love, I remind myself of Jesus' words in John 8. This is the passage where a woman is caught in adultery and the "church guys" drag her to Jesus. Can you imagine this? Truly try to put yourself in this woman's place. You've been caught in the act of sin, and now "church people" are physically taking you to the preacher for punishment. How humiliating!

These "church guys" are not kind, either, and they certainly don't have her best interest in mind. They actually are trying to put Jesus in a difficult situation. They really don't care about this woman, she is just a means to an end.

But Jesus.

No, that wasn't a typo. Those two words can stand firm just as they are. But Jesus. When Jesus enters and acts, it changes everything.

Jesus tells these men, who are bringing the woman to him, that whoever among them is without sin can cast the first stone at her. One by one they walk away. None are blameless, and therefore, none are worthy of enacting punishment upon her.

No matter how many times I read this passage, it always impacts me. I see such grace, wisdom, and love. I can imagine her widening eyes and relieved exhale as she realizes what Jesus has done for her. I can understand the overwhelming gratitude for being forgiven by Jesus. I can relate to the amazing power of His love.

Then Jesus tells her to go and leave her life of sin. He doesn't leave her in the mess in which she came. He gives her a challenge to find the way out. What's more, His mercy is the catalyst for change. There's another humbling thought. Mercy can be the catalyst for change, if we let it. For me, that change needs to happen in my own heart and attitudes. Mercy and grace and forgiveness seem to be the place to start. Even if I don't feel like it. Even if I like being frustrated. Even if I'll fail again next time.

Another relevant passage is found in Hebrews 4:15-16. It says, "For we do not have a high priest who is unable to empathize with our weaknesses, but we have one who has been tempted in every way, just as we are—yet he did not sin. Let us then approach God's throne of grace with confidence, so that we may receive mercy and find grace to help us in our time of need."

Did you catch that? It says that Jesus never sinned and therefore we can confidently approach him for mercy and grace.

What? If I had never sinned, I'm pretty sure I would not be handing out free mercy and grace. I'd be more like Lucy in *Peanuts,* setting up a help desk and charging everyone at least a nickel for my advice, and even more so, doling out judgment on everyone.

But Jesus.

Jesus has every right to withhold his mercy and grace, but he does not. When I truly remember and grasp the mercy and grace that I've been shown, it is easier for me to show grace and mercy to those I love and like.

Even if it involves my husband and GPS.

*   *   *

GPS Is Bad for Your Marriage

Originally posted on *Ten Blue Eyes* blog, April 11, 2014

I am not exaggerating to say that my husband and I have a harmonious relationship. We rarely reach the point of raising our voices with one another or driving each other insane. We are pretty laid back and get along great.

However, we've discovered a formula in our years of marriage that sets us up for spousal frustration. It's not complicated. But it is somewhat dangerous.

Kraig driving + Christy using iPhone GPS = Uh-oh.

I'm telling you, it's not all my fault. Sometimes I think the GPS lady and Kraig have schemed against me to set us all up for failure, but no one else is buying it.

I will admit, that I am directionally challenged. When receiving directions from someone I don't like to hear terms such as "head east," or "It's on the southwest corner," or "go north on the highway." These terms confuse me. If instead the GPS lady would say things like, "Turn right when you are beside Wal-Mart," or "Do you see that Applebee's up there? Great! You're going to want to slow down and make a left there," I'd be all over it. But the GPS lady never uses landmarks.

I want to help Kraig, and more importantly, I want to live and not have him get us all killed while looking at his iPhone while driving. So I take it from him and then I pass on to him what the GPS lady tells me.

Somewhere in this step of the process, things begin to break down. Sometimes that thing is me. But most of the time I don't cry. I just get us lost.

We were driving to visit my cousin who lives out of state. We had never been to her home before and so I put her address into the phone and we happily followed the little voice until it told us we had arrived at our destination. However, my cousin doesn't live in a tanning salon called Sun Your Buns.

The GPS people are out to get me.

Kraig says that I didn't put the correct address into the phone, but I think I did.

Maybe you're beginning to see our problem.

The Sun Your Buns debacle unfortunately is not the only time I've gotten hot with embarrassment. In fact, in the beautiful, sunny state of Florida, our Spousal Frustration Formula really swung into action while on a family vacation.

We were headed from Orlando to Daytona Beach. The sun shone. Kraig could sit back, relax and just drive. I had the phone in my hand and I had the address of our destination correctly entered into the phone. All was well.

I began to tell Kraig each and every turn he was to make on our ninety-minute trip to Daytona Beach.

And we made a lot of turns.

We turned into a mall parking lot and followed it around the perimeter of the mall where we came out and then entered a subdivision. We made several turns in the subdivision before entering another parking lot ... and another subdivision.

Kraig was beginning to sweat.

He was trying not to rip the phone out of my hand because I kept telling him that I was watching the GPS and this was *exactly* what the lady was telling us to do. *And* I had the address inputted correctly. *So just follow my directions!*

Kraig was really getting antsy now and telling me that he

understood I was following the directions, but when did we get on the highway that connected Orlando and Daytona Beach? "There is a highway!" he stated. "I can see the highway over there!!" "When do we get on it?" "Pleeeeeassse tell me we get on the highway!"

So I checked the phone.

"Nope. We never get on the highway."

"*What?* How can we not get on the highway? This is going to take us forever to get there on back roads! Why is it taking us on back roads? How long does it say this is going to take?"

This is when I knew we might have a problem.

I looked at the estimated time of arrival and it said we'd be in Daytona Beach in a mere two days and fourteen hours.

Maybe we should get on the highway.

Suddenly, I realized the GPS was giving me *walking* directions from Orlando to Daytona Beach. Therefore, the GPS lady with the monotone voice was kindly keeping us far away from dangerous highways and busy roads where we could get hit, and instead was directing us around mall parking lots where we'd have a nice cozy sidewalk.

Uh-oh.

So I switched it over to driving directions and told Kraig to get on the highway.

I hate GPS.

But, I love my husband, and he loves me, and he still lets me ride shotgun in the car. Sometimes he even lets me hold the iPhone.

We have a pretty harmonious relationship, Kraig and me.

If only the GPS lady would stay out of it.

*　　　*　　　*

So I don't always listen to the GPS lady. Yet, we've made it to many destinations in our married life. Granted, Kraig has probably developed an ulcer. But it's a give and take.

Listening can cause heartburn, bring heartache, or swell the heart with love. Listening can also lead you to like a person, and be liked by them. Listening validates the talker. Listening is a powerful component of any healthy and growing relationship.

Kraig once was hiring within his ministry, and asked a wise friend, who is also a ministry leader, for advice.

"I know I want to hire someone who is humble. Humility is really important, but how do you judge if a person is truly humble during interviews?" Kraig inquired.

"We look for people who are good listeners. Listening shows humility."

Such a rich response.

Listening shows humility. Wow. I have to admit that convicts me. I know many times I'd rather be the talker. I feel as if what I have to say, or what I'm going through, should be the priority in a relationship. I want the people I love and like to listen to *me*.

I get angry when Kraig does not listen to me. There are levels of this anger. The lower-level anger simmers when he's just walked in the door after work and the kids are chattering about their days and I've also asked him if it's alright if we eat in ten minutes and he hasn't responded. I can understand this. He is overwhelmed, and I will ask again. Probably in a fairly kind tone.

The next level bubbles up when I ride shotgun and he's driving again. I've told him a story about my day and asked a question. He has been watching road signs and navigating a new neighborhood. He asks me to repeat what I said because he didn't catch it all. "Say that again," is one of his common phrases in which he gently is telling me that he wasn't listening. I take a deep breath and say it again. This time he dials in his attention and responds. Kindness is forced. But it's present.

Then there's the Rolling Boil. The level of me asking him to listen while we sit in the family room and I've been waiting to run an idea past him. I have just spent dinner listening to him talk about his day, his joys, and his frustrations. It's my turn. I begin. He is playing a game on his phone. I am talking to the top of his head which is nodding slightly in an effort to fool me into thinking he's listening. But I know he's not. Kindness has left us, folks. At this point, I'm steamed. I tell him so. I envision prying the phone out of his hands, opening the back door, and heaving it into a thorny rose bush. This would take care of the GPS lady and Kraig in one swoop.

"Sorry. I was listening, but tell me again," Kraig says as he lays his phone down.

"Why can't you listen to me the first time? I just listened to you," I say in huff. "Forget it."

"No. Just tell me again."

"Forget it."

Sometimes I usher the anger out and employ the mercy I know is needed. I say it all again, and I let go of the frustration.

Other times I give up and turn on the TV.

Lest you think this only goes one way in our relationship, at times Kraig has told me something and it falls on my deaf and distracted ears. I am the one sheepishly asking him to say it once more. I am the one who has failed to show love by listening.

It happens in my friendships as well. Sometimes I realize I've been selfish and have demanded the ear of a girlfriend more than I've given her mine. But, my aim is to both listen to her heart and openly share my own.

The relationships that thrive and bring joy are the ones where the listening is mutual and balanced. We each have a turn to share, and we each feel heard. We don't use a chess timer to make sure this is happening. We just allow listening to play a key role in our friendship, and over time, it all balances out naturally.

Listening makes Love and Like loom large in our lives. (That sentence was brought to you by the letter "L.")

Listen with your ears and your heart. True listening is intent on understanding the emotions and desires behind the words. It's not listening with half of your mental capacity while the other half is forming a response. It's not listening so you can get the conversation over with faster so you can turn to your next activity, or phone, or leftover piece of cake that's been calling your name from the counter. It's listening that is seeking to truly empathize and sympathize with the talker. To show them you like or love them. To validate their words and opinions.

With this in mind, seek relationships where listening is a priority. It doesn't take more than a few short conversations to assess if someone is a good listener. Yourself included. We are not exempt from the listening criteria and goal.

If someone hasn't done a great job of listening to you, employ mercy. Repeat yourself. It's okay. You can do it. Because chances are, you're going to need to accept mercy when *you've* failed to truly listen.

Mercy and listening walk hand-in-hand. Relationships of Love and Like are even sweeter when the kindness of listening comes along for the journey.

*　　*　　*

Words are a vital component of listening. Words flow frequently in a close relationship. Many words have been spoken between Kraig and me. Some of those words heal. Some of those words hurt. And some of those words are not actually words. Let me explain that last one.

Kraig doesn't drink coffee. He thinks it tastes terrible, and he has no desire to try coffee variations in hopes of finding one he likes. He's very dubious that he'd succeed in finding any coffee pleasing to his palate. In fact, he believes it to be an impossible and pointless task.

Kraig also claims complete ignorance when it comes to the Starbucks coffee menu.

"Why don't they just say small, medium, and large like the rest of us? Why do they have to use fancy words for the sizes?"

He has asked me this several times, as if Starbucks has called and talked this reasoning through with me from their corporate headquarters.

If we do pull up to the Starbucks drive-thru speaker, and Kraig is in the driver's seat, he'll kindly order a coffee for me, but he will ask me to say the order first, and then repeat it to the speaker as if he's trying to say a security clearance phrase in Russian.

"We will take a grande flat white with cinnamon powder steamed into the milk," he says loudly, robotically, and with great articulation. For all he knows, he just ordered a can of white paint. To him, it would taste equally as delicious.

I, on the other hand, love coffee. And I associate with many coffee-drinking friends.

A few summers ago, Kraig and I were working at a Fellowship of Christian Athletes sports day camp. It required our early arrival each morning. By the fourth day, we were both pretty worn out. We had been involved with hundreds of young, energetic campers, but our own energy was waning.

I sat at the registration table with some fellow FCA volunteers, and we collectively leaned back in our chairs and sighed during an unhurried moment in the day's schedule. Kraig, who was the director of the camp, and had every right to give us orders, instead asked if he could take our orders and run to Starbucks to get us each a coffee.

He's the best. He's always thinking of others, and willing to take time and money to perk us up, even though he doesn't relate to our coffee addiction.

That's why it was really mean of me to sabotage him.

Kraig had asked if I'd take everyone's orders and then text the orders to him. He said he'd go ahead and start driving to Starbucks.

One friend's drink had the word "refresher" in it. Another ordered hers "extra hot." The terms "venti" and "latte" made it all start to sound like a silly made-up coffee language. That's when the idea started percolating in my little head.

Maybe I could add a fake order to the list. Maybe I could make that fake order sound just real enough that Kraig would say it, but just odd enough that the Starbucks employee would react.

So, I added a "mocha-schmocha-on-a-stick" to the list.

I know. It was horrible of me. So horrible, that I still barely can contain the giggles.

Kraig did, in fact, fall for the trap. He walked back into the camp some time later with cups in a cardboard drink carrier, pursed lips, and a shaking head.

"I go get you coffee, and this is the thanks I get?" he said, his eyes twinkling at mine.

"Did you actually order it?" we all asked while trying to stifle our laughter.

"Yep. I read through the orders and when I got to the mocha-schmocha-on-a-stick, the guy paused and said, 'I don't think we have that,' and I said, 'Oh, I'm pretty sure you don't.'"

We were rolling with laughter at this point. We no longer needed the caffeine to give us a boost. Picturing Kraig saying "mocha-schmocha on-a-stick" to a barista had given us all the adrenaline we needed to get through the remainder of the day.

To his credit, Kraig laughed with us.

I love that man. Even more than I love coffee.

Sometimes, our relationship is like that mocha-schmocha moment (I think I should coin that phrase; who do I call to make this happen?). We tease each other. We laugh at the other's expense. We laugh at ourselves. We do something for the other that we know isn't necessary, like buying an expensive cup of coffee, but we decide it's the way we want to say, "I love you," in that moment.

There are many ways to say, "I love you."

Kraig shows me he loves me by actually saying the words, "I love you." He does this almost every time we talk on the phone before he hangs up. We never made the decision to do this, it just happened. It's an unspoken agreement about speaking our love for one another. I have come to expect it, count on it, and find such joy in those three words at the end of a phone call.

When Kraig says them, and I know he's in the presence of a coworker in the boardroom, or family member on the golf course, or the receptionist at the dentist office, it makes me feel like I'm his priority over their reactions. That his love for me is more important to him than looking "macho" in front of the guys, or "mushy" in front of the secretary. Those three words carry much weight and I am so grateful for their impact.

As important as "I love you" is in a relationship, "I like you" is vital too. There are also many ways to say, "I like you." They require effort and intentionality.

Sometimes, knowing Kraig still likes me, as well as loves me, refreshes like a deep breath of fresh air. Like when you didn't realize you were holding your breath, and then something triggers you to inhale long and deeply through your nose and you hold that air in your lungs for a few seconds and you feel so much better. (You just did that, didn't you? You took a really deep breath while reading that paragraph. It's okay, you can admit it.)

Words and actions that display Love and Like can be like oxygen to the soul. They can also knock the wind out of you. It can go either way, and when it goes poorly, it really hurts. When those words or actions are coming from someone you happen to like, or love, it's the worst.

I've said it before, and I'll say it again, whoever coined the phrase "Sticks and stones can break my bones but words can never hurt me," was basically a moron. They need to get their paperwork to the courthouse and un-coin that phrase, and while they're there, they can get me the phone number I need to expedite my mocha-schmocha idea.

Or ... words can be helpful. We often tell children to "use your words." How about you? How can you use *your* words this week? Today? Tell someone something that will encourage them. Even if you don't get a kind comment in return. Even if they don't show you Love or Like in any form. Do it anyway.

Tell your husband he's a good man. Tell your neighbor she's an amazing gardener. Tell the mom at Target with the tantrum-throwing toddler that she's doing just fine. Be specific. Be genuine. "You did a good job leading the meeting today." "You're a good mom for telling your child they can't eat candy for dinner." "You're a good mom even when you do let your kid eat a lollipop at dinner." Sometimes, we all need a little sweetness in our day.

Maybe you can be that sweet treat for someone else. Just by using your words.

*   *   *

One problem with words and actions in relationships is that they can be so subjective. Filtered through experience, personality and opinions, intended meanings change in our very ears.

When our son, Karson, turned ten, we held a birthday party for him in the backyard and invited three of his close friends. The boys were playing various sports, and of course, trying to beat each other in each. At one point, they were hitting foam golf balls with a real iron golf club and trying to see who could get the ball closest to the designated target. Our nephew, Kamron, stood a little too close during a friend's backswing, and got clobbered in the head with the golf club.

Kraig and I watched this play out. No blood gushed, and Kamron seemed fine, so we did not go running to the scene. But we listened to the boys handle it.

"Are you okay, Kamron?" they asked. "Do you have a concussion?"

Kamron rubbed his head and said he was fine.

Max thought he'd make sure that he was still thinking straight, so he asked a question to determine if Kamron had a concussion.

"Who is the best football team in the AFC?"

Kamron looked at Max, who was an avid Pittsburgh Steelers fan. Kamron also happened to be a big Pittsburgh fan (ironic since we live in Indiana).

"The Steelers!"

"He's fine!" Max yelled.

Kraig and I laughed. We tried to explain that you shouldn't ask a subjective question when testing for a concussion. It happened to work out this time, because we had two Steelers fans collaborating, but normally, it's better to ask an objective question like, "Who is the President of the United States?"

The boys didn't really care. They were back to golfing.

So, maybe you've been hurt by someone you love or like. Maybe their subjective words hurt you. Maybe they accidently hit you in their backswing.

The subjective quality of human nature can cause trouble. Sometimes we see the same thing through two different lenses, and sometimes, we have the same lens and still disagree. Either way, disagreeing can be difficult. Concussion or not.

I've been hurt by a friend's comment, only to find out later, after wasting much time feeling down, that I had taken the comment out of context, or misunderstood her intent.

I hope it's not the case, but I'm guessing I've hurt friends with comments that came across wrong. It makes my heart hurt, but I know it's bound to happen.

It helps to put the comments of others through the filter of history, especially if the comment hurt us. What do I know to be true about this person? Is this hurtful comment consistent with her character? Is she aiming to hurt me? Would she desire to hurt me? Am I just understanding this comment out of context? Sometimes, we just need to apply some common sense.

Recently, I bought some new tea called "Sleepytime." It is an herbal blend that aims to help calm you before bed. Kraig didn't know we owned this tea, and I forgot about that fact when I told him, one evening, that I was going to "go make some Sleepytime." He looked at me as if I were insane. He ran this comment through his history filter. It was not a hurtful comment, but one that he did not understand, and he thought it seemed out of character for me. Kraig was confused. I was also confused by his response, because me making a cup of hot tea before bed was not an upsetting action, or an unusual one at that.

Turns out that Kraig thought I was talking in a "baby language" and telling him I was going to bed! When he found out Sleepytime was, in fact, the name of my tea, and when I understood that he thought I was talking to him as if he were a toddler, we both had a good laugh! "I'm going to go make some Sleepytime" is now an accepted phrase in our home for "I'm going to bed!" An inside joke that I've now let you in on. You're welcome.

Speaking of jokes, laughter is another great tool for the conflicts found in Love and Like. Truly, laughter is a great addition to almost anything! In our relationships, we can work hard to employ mercy and grace and forgiveness, and to actively listen, but we shouldn't stop there. Relationships require work, but they should also include joy! Without delight in your Love and Like, then relationships are just another task, like vacuuming your car mats, shoveling the driveway, or emptying the dishwasher.

I mentioned Mephibosheth in the Guilt and Regret chapter and how King David showed him great kindness because of his father Jonathan. This was because Jonathan and David were very close friends. We are told they liked each other and loved each other. (1 Samuel 18:3) Jonathan's father, Saul, hated David and literally tried to kill him (awkward) and yet the two men remained loyal friends. Their friendship literally spared David's life, when Jonathan warned him of his father's plan to kill him and helped him escape. (1 Samuel 20) Their friendship also gave them each delight, and hope, and joy. It is a friendship so strong and impactful, that it is mentioned as part of David's story in the Bible. Bigger than an aside, it was central and life-giving, part of what made David who he was. The bond they shared was beautiful. This tells me close relationships, Love and Like, are blessings. They are meant to be tended and nurtured, but they also are meant to be enjoyed.

God is the one who created Love and Like in the first place.

1 John 4:19 says, "We love because He first loved us."

Love and Like are gifts from God. Just as my relationship with God Himself takes effort on my part to grow in my knowledge of Him (reading the Bible and studying it) and in my love for Him (talking to Him, worshiping Him), it also gives me amazing joy and delight. We are designed to Love and Like God Himself!

God created us because He wants to be in an intimate relationship with us. Mankind ruined that by sinning, but God offers a way to redeem us from sin and death and to restore each of us to Him. If we so accept it.

We don't have to wait until Heaven to know God and be in a close relationship with Him, we can know Him and find joy and comfort in His love now! He wants to know me. Like me. Because He loves me. Because He loves you. What really blows my mind is that God doesn't require me to be "likeable" or "loveable" before He extends this grace to me. No, He reached out and made a way for redemption while I was still an ugly mess.

"But Got demonstrated His own love for us in this: While we were still sinners, Christ died for us." (Romans 5:8)

While we were still sinners. While we were not, and are not, easy to love, or naturally likeable, God chose to sacrifice His Son's life for us. Because we are worth it to Him. Because He wants to have a relationship with each one of us. Love and Like mean that much to Him.

By God authoring Love and Like, we can now reap the benefits and joy they provide! Not only with God Himself, which is the greatest gift of all, but with each other on this Earth.

Even as I sit and type these words, my phone keeps dinging, indicating I am receiving texts. I'm in a text thread with some girlfriends. The conversation is always flowing, even if we go days without saying anything. But, sometimes, the text ding rings constantly. When I am deep in thought, I turn to look at these texts anyway. Why? Because they are life-giving to me. The words of these women make me laugh. They make me think. They make me feel hope and love. It takes work from each of us to continue the relationship, but the delight and joy we receive makes it worth the effort!

A garden takes toil and effort to tend, but then you have the satisfying reward of the harvest. The delight of a carrot snapping between your front teeth. The sweet corn you canned and enjoy in the winter months. Love and Like take toil and effort, but they can bring great delight to the soul.

My friendships are worth the effort. My marriage is worth the effort. Love and Like is worth the effort!

From the toil of Love and Like, from the work of giving mercy, showing grace, offering forgiveness, and listening humbly, we can reap a harvest of sweet laughter and joy.

*   *   *

Slice of Hope: Healthy relationships require effort. From the toil of giving mercy, showing grace, offering forgiveness, and listening humbly, we can reap a harvest of sweet laughter and joy.

five

loss and anger

I could not allow my son to succeed.

Not in this game of balloon volleyball. Not in my living room.

I gritted my teeth and raised my left hand high. I knew this was the moment. Whatever transpired in the next few seconds would seal the deal. Defeat crouched at the door, but I was pushing against it, willing victory to come forth instead.

The first team to ten points would be the winning pair. My middle child, Karly, and I were losing. Our opponents? My oldest child, twelve-year-old Karson, and Kenzie, the baby of the family, who was not so little anymore, at the age of seven. This stage of parenting offered more competition and group participation. No one was benched due to diapers or claiming they didn't understand the rules.

The couch served as our wide and somewhat obtrusive "net." The pale blue balloon that we were using as our "volleyball" hung in the air, suspended as if taking in the scene for itself.

If you could have frozen the moment and spread the image between your thumb and forefinger to zoom in on the details, perhaps you would have seen two opposing characters sitting on my shoulders like in the old cartoons.

On my right shoulder sits "The Mom." She's sweet, and gentle, and whispering things in my ear like, "Let your kids win. That's what good moms do." And, "Encourage these three dear children for the skill level they each possess."

But the whispers of this dear woman were being drowned out by the character on my left shoulder, the "You're Not As Young And Athletic As You Think You Are" Woman. This chick resembled the thirty-nine-year-old version of me yet still thinks she's sixteen. She's wearing her blue Umbro shorts and white Mizuno volleyball shoes from the early 90s, and she's not taking "loss" for an answer. She's on her feet shouting, "It's game point, for heaven's sake! Put your back into it!" "You can't let these offspring beat you in a game you played in high school! Step up and crush it!"

Sadly, this overzealous voice won out, because as the balloon slowly drifted downward above the couch, I smacked it with my left hand as hard as I could. My son did the same. As we hit the balloon, it gave up. It popped, and its limp, slimy blue corpse fell to the ground.

Seven-year-old Kenzie began to cry. We'd popped her precious balloon.

Karson shrugged.

I winced in pain and slouched onto the "net" while holding my left hand against my body.

The nausea hit next.

Are you serious? I thought. *Did I just break my finger?*

I looked at my hand. My ring finger already was beginning to swell.

I raised my eyes to Karson. "The Mom" voice urged me to make sure he was all right. He was. He said he barely felt the impact.

But I felt the impact. Even more than the balloon.

I retreated to the bathroom and sat in front of the toilet. Oh, the thrill of victory and the agony of feeling like you're going to throw up because you just got injured while playing with a balloon!

"What's going on?" my husband yelled from the other room. Moments later he stood in the bathroom doorway, looking at me as if trying to solve a puzzle on *Wheel of Fortune* before the buzzer sounded. There were missing details in his mind, and this wasn't making sense.

"I hurt my finger," I mustered as beads of sweat formed on my forehead and rolled down my back.

Kraig raised his eyebrows as the kids' voices excitedly filled him in on the details.

I took several deeps breaths and looked down at my hand once again. I needed to act. My wedding rings were growing tighter by the second. They had better come off.

I wiggled my engagement ring and slowly moved it over my middle knuckle and off my finger. Immediately I tried to do the same with my wedding band. It wouldn't budge. I could turn it from side to side, but I could not pull it over my now very swollen knuckle.

I rose with the grace of an elderly giraffe, and walked to the kitchen. "Kraig, can you please call Laura and tell her I can't walk with her this evening?" I was supposed to go for a walk with a friend, but the thought made me even more nauseated. Kraig shook his head, but dialed the phone and fulfilled his marriage vows of "in sickness and in health, and in finger injuries which cause acute nausea," by explaining to my friend that I had to cancel our walk due to a finger injury.

The next few hours involved ice and throbbing. I barely slept that night.

"Would you make fun of me if I went to the doctor today about

113

my finger?" I asked Kraig the next morning over the phone. He was at the office, and by mid-morning, I longed for relief.

"I think you probably just jammed it and the swelling will go down in three or four days. You can just keep icing it."

"I know," I whimpered, "but my wedding ring is so tight now. I can't even spin it anymore and my finger is throbbing. I wouldn't be as anxious to go see a doctor if it weren't for the ring, but...."

"Well, if that's how you want to spend your time today, I guess I don't care."

The romance was palpable.

"Kraig! It's not about how I want to spend my time!"

"Well, I guess we have met our deductible, so if you really want to go, go."

We should have included something about compassion and mercy in our wedding vows.

It turns out I was right to see a doctor that day. In fact, the doctor said that had I waited much longer, I most likely would have lost my finger due to the loss of circulation from the wedding ring. My finger was blue within a few centimeters of its tip.

"You can pick," the doctor said. "Keep the ring, or keep the finger."

"I'll go with the finger," I said as I signed a waiver stating they could cut my wedding band off.

As I walked out to the parking lot with my mutilated wedding band in a plastic bag, my finger in a splint, and my hand in an ace bandage, I dialed my husband.

"It's a good thing I came to the doctor today. Let's just say you could have had a nine-fingered wife."

To his credit, he admitted I was right, and he was wrong. He expressed his condolences for my wedding band, and for the fact that I had actually not jammed my finger, but fractured my middle knuckle and would now have to attend finger therapy to learn to bend it once again.

Finger therapy.

I've discovered there are two words you can put together in the English language with laughter directly resulting: "finger" and "therapy." But, they say laughter is the best medicine. That, and being right. Not that I'm competitive at all.

Winning comes in many forms.

I think that's in our wedding vows somewhere too.

*   *   *

I never used to think of myself as competitive. Sure, I competed in sports as a teenager, and always wanted to be, and do, my best, but I wasn't "ruined" if we lost a game. I had a fairly good perspective on life priorities. At least, that's how I remember it.

But lately, let's say for the past decade, I've noticed a competitive nature rising to the surface. Maybe I have a good perspective on life priorities, but I like to win, too. So, if I can do both, why not?

The balloon volleyball game and resulting comments I'd make to people who heard about the story, "Well, I might have broken my finger, but I didn't lose the volleyball game!" led me to hear my own warped desire to succeed.

I can't put my finger on the reason. I even completed and passed finger therapy, folks. But, we didn't work on puzzling questions such as these.

Here's what I can tell you. I don't like to lose. I also have a fairly healthy perspective on what's important in life. I want to win, but I usually want to do it with a good attitude, and healthy relationships intact.

That's why, when I faced a seemingly lose-only situation—which involved important life priorities, and my husband—I had a very difficult time.

*   *   *

Little girls, and even big girls, dream about their wedding days and future children. At least I did. Many of my friends did too.

As baby-faced elementary kids, we'd play Barbies in our bedrooms and imagine the most elaborate scenarios. Barbie and Ken falling head-over-plastic-high-heels in love. The well-dressed, if not stiff-jointed, children we'd add to their family, and cram into the backseat of the Barbie car. Invariably there were twins, cute and well-behaved.

As acne-faced preteens, we began to notice actual breathing boys, and we wondered if we'd marry anyone from science class or the cafeteria. Several of my friends practiced writing their first names accompanied with the last name of the boys on whom they had crushes. This was done with many loops and curls, and doodled hearts.

But when it came to dreaming about our future families, as fresh-faced college freshmen, the stakes were higher. Though they were mostly a few years older than us, real girls were getting engaged to real boys with real rings and real jobs. The conversations about future children happened most at this phase. They weren't frequent; we mostly focused on other priorities, like classes, our hair, and actually finding a guy. But they did happen.

"How many kids do you want to have?" one of us would ask.

The answers would vary. Some wanted two. Some ten. Some weren't sure they wanted kids at all. Me? I always said the same thing. An indefinite "two, or three, or four."

"I used to think I wanted two or three, but after tutoring the four Justice kids, I think I might want four," I explained. The Justice family had asked me to visit their home a couple of times a week and tutor their children in Spanish and art. Their kids were well-behaved, adorable, and I got paid to hang out with them. What's not to like about four kids?

Thus the question, "How many kids do I want?" entered my mind. Like I said, I wasn't married (or even dating anyone) at this point, but the wheels of decision had begun to turn.

Now, as a married mother, I find it quite funny that I thought then that I could actually control this. I thought choosing how many kids I wanted was about as easy as deciding how many cherry tomatoes I added to my salad in the dining commons. Two, or three … or maybe four today.

Because when I did get married two years after college, I did marry an actual breathing (if not stiff-jointed) man. He's a keeper and the answer to my prayers, and I most certainly enjoy writing my first name alongside his last name. The alliteration of Christy Cabe makes me happier than it probably should.

Nonetheless, Kraig and I were in love. New, sweet, romantic, blissful love. We rarely argued, and we were almost always on the "same page" on decisions. Some of this is due to our personalities. We're both very laid back and mild-natured. So, when Kraig and I talked about how many kids we wanted, we both happily agreed that "two, or three, or four," was a good answer. We'd just see what happened and go from there.

As I shared in my book, *Brownie Crumbs and Other Life Morsels*, we did have children. A son first, and then two devastating miscarriages, followed by a shocking and heartbreaking cancer diagnosis of our then toddler son, Karson. Life threw us some major curve balls. It was awful. Then, in the midst of three years of Karson's chemotherapy, our daughters, Karly, and Kenzie, were born. It was a crazy season of life.

The combination of spinal taps, chemotherapy, a chubby bald head, a newborn, a *tiny* bald head, steroid rage, prophylactic antibiotics, another newborn, a "no-mo chemo" party, a cancer-free status, and sending a then five-year-old Karson to kindergarten while pushing a three-month-old and an almost two-year-old in a stroller to the bus stop nearly killed me (the whole season nearly killed me, not just the walk to the bus stop, lest you think I'm that out of shape.) There were so many emotions. *So many.* When I think of 2010, when our youngest was born seven days after Karson's last chemo dose, and when my husband took a job promotion which brought greater responsibility, and when I sent my immunosuppressed child to public school on a yellow bus, I sometimes just shake my head in shock we actually made it to 2011. But we did.

Life marched on, and so did we.

During those first couple of years after having Kenzie (our third child), I believed I was "done" having kids. In fact, with all of the stress and change and emotion of those years, I was pretty certain another pregnancy and child would be the tipping point. A tipping point into insanity, or rage, or depression, or ... I don't even know what. But I knew I was at my limit.

Kraig, on the other hand, could have added another child at this point. Granted, he did not have to go through the actual nine months of swollen ankles, heartburn, weight gain, and hormone sabotage. So to him, adding one more little bundle of love to our already chaotic nest seemed doable. He never pushed me to add another child, he was simply willing, and not at all opposed to the idea.

I was opposed.

But then we moved to a bigger house with a basement and great backyard, and several weeks later, Kenzie turned two. We celebrated on the back patio with an M&M's themed party. In the weeks and months to come, something changed in me. I suddenly had more space. Not just in my closets and bedrooms, but in my heart. I watched my baby turn into a toddler and chase after her big brother and sister in the driveway, and I ached. Because I love babies. And I didn't have one anymore.

Life had hit its rhythm as a family of five. We weren't just surviving anymore, we were thriving. I started to allow my mind to replay the question once again. "How many kids do I want?"

*　　　*　　　*

I surprised myself. My thoughts turned to adding another child to our family more often than I expected. My desire for another baby was growing right along with my three children's hands and feet. They were losing the cute "baby fat" on the back of their hands and their toes kept pushing out to the ends of their shoes. They certainly were not going to stay little forever. Or even for long. Was I ready to move out of this stage of parenting and into the "big kid" stage?

Then one day, I had a suspicion. I felt pregnant. As with all of my other pregnancies, I read my body's signals correctly. I was indeed pregnant. I told Kraig my suspicion early in the day, but didn't take a pregnancy test until evening. I then verified the news with Kraig in a rather anticlimactic way. I flat out told him while he sat in the recliner in the family room, and then his phone rang with a work call. He answered it. We didn't even have a moment to soak in the news together or discuss it.

Perhaps it made sense for Kraig to answer the phone, and for me to deliver the news without fanfare, but I sensed maybe Kraig wasn't sure how to respond, and his ringing phone gave him a great diversion. It gave me a diversion too. One long enough to plop into the other recliner and stew.

I was miffed Kraig answered the phone. I was surprised I had actually gotten pregnant. I was happy. I was anxious. My emotions ran all over the map.

The thought of holding a new baby and staring at its tiny toes made me warm. The visions of my own body changing in the coming months made me cringe. And our family dynamic. What would this do to the rhythm and balance we'd found together as a unit of five?

I was older now than I had been with my other pregnancies, and in fact, at thirty-five, I was considered "old" when it came to pregnancy. "Advanced Maternal Age" they call it. How lovely.

Kraig was older yet. With our age gap of four and a half years, he was just a few weeks shy of turning forty. And, forty loomed large.

I had always pictured us being done with the baby stage by the time we hit forty. But, I was still four and a half years away from the milestone, and Kraig didn't seem forty, so I figured it would be fine.

Kraig was less enthused. He didn't have a problem with turning forty. He took it in stride and in his typical practical and steady manner. But, several times he mentioned that he never pictured having a newborn after he turned forty. Whereas I was not ready for a fourth child in the first couple of years after Kenzie's birth, and Kraig was, now we had switched. He was feeling done, and I was ready for a fourth.

The facts were pointing to a fourth, due in a little less than nine months. Kraig said it would take him a bit to get used to the idea of adding another baby now, but that he was happy and okay with it. He just needed time to process the information.

A few weeks later, to celebrate his big birthday, the two of us (well, two and a half) went to dinner at Outback Steakhouse and we discussed life. We'd had a few weeks to process and accept the facts. We had both now mostly settled into the idea of a fourth child, but we were the only ones. I was about eight weeks pregnant now, and we'd told no one. We wanted to wait until the first ultrasound at ten weeks, and then tell our kids first. We knew they would be ecstatic! In fact, dreaming about telling our kids that another brother or sister was on his or her way excited me most, other than the baby itself.

Over our steaks and fries, we talked about telling the kids at the big family birthday party the first weekend of October, which was just two weeks away. We'd tell the kids after school on Friday, so they could hear it first, and then we'd tell the extended family that evening. It would be so fun. We knew everyone would be surprised, but delighted. I planned to give my mom some photo collages of our kids for her birthday (which was one of the several birthdays we'd be celebrating) and I hoped to have a good picture of our ultrasound to frame and wrap up as way of our announcement. The anticipation brought a smile to my face.

Overall, Kraig seemed more at ease with the facts now too, though He made multiple references to his age and he did a lot of math problems, adding up how old he'd be at the baby's high school graduation, college graduation, and how many years he or she would be home with us alone after Kenzie turned eighteen.

The numbers made my head spin. Or maybe that was the hormones. Either way, questions kept going around and around in my mind. How old would "Number Four" be when *I* turned forty? Would that seem weird to other people? Would I be considered an "old Mom?"

Then, crazy, irrational questions began to overwhelm me. Things I knew were just plain stupid to dwell on and be concerned about, but they weighed me down nonetheless. Questions like, "How can we add a sixth person to our family when our Christmas stocking holders spell the word 'Peace,' and that's only a five-letter word?" I spent more time than I'd like to admit mulling this question over. Could I add a star? An exclamation point! Would six holders fit on the mantle, anyway?

What about the van? Who would sit in which seat and how many car seats and/or booster seats would we be dealing with at a time? Would the kids fight over the back seat?

The kitchen table. We'd have to rearrange our usual spots to put a highchair on the end where there is the most space. How will the other kids feel about sitting in a new spot?

Going out to eat. We'd never fit in a booth with six people. We'd be stuck at a table for years. I like booths better.

At least we'd have an even number of people for rollercoaster rides. I actually had people tell me that an even number was good for this very reason. Our theme park balance would be in check. That was a relief.

The crazy thoughts kept coming. I knew they were fairly light topics in the big scheme of things, but they still weighed heavily.

I also grew more and more obsessed with the idea of "Number Four." I finally had a definite answer to the question of, "How many kids do you want?"

I wanted four children.

*   *   *

I had been waiting for this day for weeks. The party was scheduled for later that evening, and the ultrasound for right after lunch. I was so excited to see the fuzzy, grey images of our next child on the ultrasound monitor. Mostly, I couldn't wait to tell the kids.

Nausea still hit me from time to time, and I believed the morning sickness was a good sign. Having been through two miscarriages after our first child was born, I was very sensitive to my body's signals. Things were going well this time. I had been extra tired during the day and had taken some catnaps. I also had aversions to certain smells and food. The fresh

122

seafood case at the grocery store about did me in every time. That, and dog and cat food commercials made me gag.

I asked my friend, Whitney, to babysit my girls, who were ages three and five, and I met Kraig for lunch before the ultrasound. Karson, our oldest child, was in third grade and at school. I told Whitney that Kraig and I were having a day date, and I didn't mention the appointment. It had been hard keeping the pregnancy from her, and I was so excited about my plan to finally tell her when I picked up my girls later that afternoon.

The ultrasound tech welcomed us and everything proceeded as usual.

And then it didn't.

The tech was quiet as she found the baby on the screen. There was no visible movement. My throat grew tight and my heart raced. Why couldn't I see the baby's heartbeat? I'd been through multiple ultrasounds like this one, and though I'm not a doctor, I had a good idea of what I should be seeing on the screen.

After several more attempts to locate life, the tech finally said, "I'm sorry, there isn't a heartbeat."

Though I'd had a few moments to come to this realization on my own, the news stunned me. How could this be? I was further along than my other miscarriages by several weeks. I was feeling nauseated, and tired, and pregnant.

"The baby is only measuring at seven or eight weeks," the tech continued. "It seems to have stopped developing a couple of weeks ago. I'm so sorry."

My head sank further into the pillow like a 300-pound anchor. I strained to slowly turn it away from the screen and toward the face of my husband. He looked surprised and seemed at a loss for words.

"I'll give you a minute, and then you can meet with your doctor to talk about next steps," the tech said as she left the room.

I didn't cry. Not yet. Instead I mechanically moved through the next hour of discussing things with the doctor and going home.

I stopped at Whitney's to get the girls. I had desperately wanted to tell her the good news, but now my somber mood led to me telling her about my crushing disappointment. She pulled me out into her garage and hugged me and prayed for me as our children, oblivious to our news, played loudly inside.

That night at the party, I didn't say a word about it. I didn't want to take away from the joy. It was like I was living in an out-of-body experience. I totally disconnected from the facts. I went on as if nothing had happened, and I continued that way for the following two days.

At some point that weekend, I did tell our families that I had been pregnant and that the baby had no heartbeat at our ten-week ultrasound. I told them how sad I was, and that I'd require a surgery to complete the miscarriage on Monday morning. But I was still in a robotic, fairly non-emotional state.

Sunday, two days after the ultrasound, our church broke ground for a new children's wing. Since I had served on staff at the church as the Director of Children's Ministries years before, and because I had attended the church as a child myself (my dad became the pastor there when I was ten years old), I was asked to pray at the dedication service. So, I did. Though I was scheduled to drop our kids off that evening at my parents and get to the hospital before dawn the next morning for a D & C procedure (to clear my womb), I didn't make that known, and I attended the service and prayed as planned. The irony of the moment was not lost on me, though. There I was, helping to break ground and dedicate a new addition for children, when my own new addition had no life inside of me.

As I often do, I had first sought Kraig's wisdom and opinion. He is one of the wisest people I've ever met, and that is a blessing to me, as I often benefit from his advice. So, I had asked Kraig before deciding if I should still participate in the dedication service. He encouraged me to go through with my involvement. I leaned on his support and found comfort to get through it knowing he was there with me. Most did not know my inward pain, but knowing that he did was enough. His arm gently around my shoulders, or his hand reaching for mine, amidst the crowd of noisy people, were the breaths of fresh air I needed for my panting soul.

After the service, we dropped the kids off at Mom's and Dad's, and we called a local Mexican restaurant to order takeout. On our way to pick it up, we stopped at an outdoor Redbox kiosk to rent a movie. We were going to make a date night out of this evening.

Then it happened. My body caught up with what my mind already knew. It abruptly decided, in the parking lot of Walgreens in front of the Redbox, that it was ready to accept the fact the baby was no longer alive, and let go of the pregnancy. Now.

Much bleeding and pain led us to call the doctor and head straight to the ER. We never did pick up our takeout. Kraig stopped by later in the week to offer to pay for the forgotten food.

At the ER, after long hours of pain and blood loss, that neared the point of being too much blood loss, an emergency surgery was warranted. It couldn't wait until morning.

I had to sign forms that I could be given blood if needed. The pen felt heavy in my pale hand.

The on-call doctor, whom I had never met, walked in and said, "I just want you to know this is not your fault. You did nothing to cause this. If it were that easy to end a pregnancy on your own, then there wouldn't be such a thing as abortion clinics."

I found this statement to be comforting and disturbing at the same time. I was fading fast in my energy and mental clarity, and I appreciated the doctor's attempt to ease any sense of guilt, yet I struggled to take it all in at that moment.

Soon I was waking up in the recovery room and shivering under five heated blankets. My body shook. It was a physical reaction to the anesthesia, but also a symbolic picture of what was to come as far as my emotional and spiritual state. Shook.

Kraig was by my side and discussing the heated blankets with a nurse. "Can she get another blanket?" he asked. "She still seems cold." Later, when I was finally discharged, he drove me through the twenty-four-hour pharmacy drive-thru. He made sure I had everything I needed.

We got home in the middle of the night, and I crawled into our bed, where I stayed for hours and hours.

Though we had already scheduled to have a new roof put on our house the following day, and with our bedroom being on the second floor where the pounding and voices of the men working above me were loud and clear, I slept. I didn't care. I could hear the nails being driven, the shingles being dragged across the slope, and the crew singing, "I can see clearly now the rain is gone...."

Yet I lay there. My body was sore and exhausted. I was in much need of rest, but my thoughts and my feelings were active.

My emotions now entered the scene with force. I recognized most of them from my previous miscarriages and other losses. Sadness. Disappointment. Shock. Denial. But, a new emotion I'd not experienced much arrived. Anger.

Pure, hot, anger.

It rose up in me, an uninvited foreigner seeking a place to settle. It found vacancy in my heart and mind.

I let God have it. I'd been through enough, and now God had

taken this baby from me. I had decided I wanted a fourth child. Didn't God know that? Of course He did! So why did He allow this to happen? I wanted that baby desperately. And He'd taken it away.

What was more, my sense of entitlement fueled my anger. I deserved this one. I'd already experienced loss in my life with the death of my mother when I was in fifth grade, two miscarriages, and a toddler son who went through cancer. Wasn't that enough, God?

Even more, I had handled this pregnancy in the "right way." Instead of being filled with worry about miscarrying, I had chosen to trust God. Yes, I had worried about silly things like our Christmas stocking holders, but I exhibited trust in God for the baby's life. I had patiently waited to tell our children to make it all as perfect as possible, and now, with the surgery and my recovery, we'd decided to tell them the sad news instead, and it broke my heart.

I was mad.

I didn't care to move past the anger. No. I had set up camp with this new emotional guest, and I planned to stay awhile.

*   *   *

Tears flowed often. I didn't do much to hide or stop them, either. At the dinner table, my three precious kids saw my raw sadness. They ached too. They had wanted a baby to join our family as well. They had come so close, and we all wept over the sibling and son or daughter we'd never meet this side of Heaven.

My kids' presence was a great comfort to me. Their hugs, pats on my back, and sweet hands on my arm or shoulder soothed like a balm to me, but though it helped cover the sadness, it did not take it away.

Comments made by family or friends who meant well, but who

would have been better off staying silent, fell painfully on my ears. "At least you already have three children." Or, the more common, "You can still have another baby." These statements may have been true, but in my mind, they diminished the loss of the baby I'd just carried for over ten weeks. I would never dream of saying, "You can get married again," to a widow who'd just suffered the loss of her husband. Of course not!

My own father remarried less than a year after my mom's death, and I was one who encouraged him to do so, but that's not the point. I wouldn't have dismissed my dad's pain (or obviously my own!) to jump right to the pursuit of his remarriage without acknowledging the pain of our loss first. No! Grieving the loss of my mom was expected and necessary. It's absolutely acceptable and wise to grieve the loss of a loved one. It's one of the most expected human responses I can think of. But for some reason, with miscarriage, it's different.

Maybe it's because the loved one is unknown to virtually everyone else but the one who carried it. For whatever reason, it seems expected that the woman quickly gloss over the loss and recover. The timing of such comments to a grieving mommy-not-to-be-anymore is brutal. I wasn't in the right state of mind to correct or refute any of these statements in the days or weeks after my loss. I didn't have the will to do so, at least not outside my own cranium.

I sat around a lot. Partly, due to the fact I was still recovering from a rough surgery, but mostly because I lacked the motivation and desire to do much else.

One day, Kraig was working in the garage rearranging things and trying to organize our mess. Three children and their bikes, scooters, helmets, not to mention the basketballs, whiffle ball bats, golf clubs, sidewalk chalk, and such, made for quite a pile of chaos. I'm not sure if Kraig's goal was more to organize the mess, or to get out of the house and away from my mood, even if only as far as the garage.

I found him there, and settled on the thinly carpeted concrete step. I wasn't comfortable in any sense.

And then the floodgates opened. I told Kraig about my anger. As if he didn't already know. I spilled my feelings of entitlement and frustration. I told him how I'd tried so hard to handle this pregnancy in a godly way, and look where it got me. I whined and wailed over the loss and seethed through my teeth with anger.

Kraig turned and looked at me. He was holding the yellow broom he'd been sweeping the garage with, and he leaned on the handle and said, "It seems to me like you think you deserved this baby, and you didn't. None of us deserve anything. Everything we have is a gift from God. You couldn't have earned this baby by not worrying, or by suffering enough. As difficult as that may sound."

Believe me, it sounded difficult! Those words had come from the man I was married to, and who had lost the same baby I had.

Let me tell you what can put a strain between a husband and a wife. The loss of a dream, a miscarriage, rampant hormones, and a husband telling his wife she can't claim entitlement to appease her anger.

The anger inside of me grew. It now encompassed Kraig, as well as God.

Our conversations did not end with a kiss. Or even a hug. It also did not end with a gentle, "Let me think that over, honey," or even a "Let's talk about this more later."

It ended with anger piled upon an existing heap of smoldering anger.

And an empty garage step.

*   *   *

Slice of Hope: Sometimes we pray and live through gritted teeth. Continue anyway.

six

lamenting
and living

Nine days. That's how long, after my surgery to complete my third and most recent miscarriage, I stayed angry and cynical toward God. And toward Kraig, for that matter. For me, it was an eternity.

Whereas I am usually one to perform spiritual checks and balances on myself to make sure I'm in tune with God and His Word, this time, without much checking, I knew I wasn't. But, I didn't care. That I knew I was out of sorts spiritually, and yet didn't desire to fix it, was so out of character for me that I almost didn't recognize myself.

Then I found comfort, relief, and the permission I needed to begin the restoration process at the most likely and unlikely place. Church.

I'd attended church my entire life, and it has been one of the catalysts most responsible for my spiritual growth, second only to my family. But, I was still stewing, and not wishing to give church the pleasure of cooling the heat. I had wanted a baby, not a sermon.

That fall morning, just nine days after the devastating ultrasound, the sermon arrived in the form of music and clarity that poured into my soul.

A band called the Sons of Korah, based out of Australia, was visiting the States and performing a concert at our church.

Our church rarely held this kind of service on a Sunday morning. It was music with a side of preaching instead of the usual vice versa. This way, the congregation could sample the band's music before their evening concert at our church. It struck the perfect chord with me.

The Sons of Korah take Scripture, specifically the Psalms, and put it to music. Straightforward Bible verses set to song. No added choruses or repeated lines, other than what was written in the first place. That October morning, they sang a collection of psalms that are known as laments.

Lamenting was something I could get behind.

I listened as they sang the wailing and mourning words of David from the Old Testament. I knew about this David guy. This is the kind king who helped his best friend's crippled son, Mephibosheth. He was the great-grandson of Ruth, and one of Israel's greatest leaders. I'd studied David's life, but it wasn't until that morning that I understood his lamenting.

As the Sons of Korah sang his words, David's anger and pain sounded so familiar to my suffering heart. I took it in like breath, but I didn't yet allow it to ease my physical posture. I sat with my arms crossed tightly across my chest. My lips sealed, my eyes moist. My ears open.

God helped me to understand something as those words of lament washed over me in song. For the past nine days, I had believed that my emotions had been completely wrong, that they were broken, or that I needed a sign taped to my head and heart that read "out of order."

I knew it was normal to feel the emotions of sadness, fear, disappointment, and shock, but my anger had caused a disturbance I didn't think was permissible.

Now I wasn't so sure. David, a man that God Himself calls a "man after my own heart" (Acts 13:22), apparently not only felt anger, but expressed it. He even wrote it down and sang about it. His anger was legit.

As real, and deep, and simmering as mine was.

Lamenting was a tool God gave David to express his feelings and to understand the depth of his grief. David's mourning and lamenting over his own sins of adultery and murder led him to redemption. (2 Samuel 11-12) A truly powerful example of a life saved and completely changed by God's grace and restoration.

The band's musicians spoke between the songs, and their explanation of David's state of mind and bitter words rang true.

I was listening.

David didn't stop living while he lamented. He lamented while he continued to live, while he continued to move forward. I felt like I was given permission that morning to lament as I lived in my grief, anger, and sadness.

After the service, while in the hallway picking our children up from their Sunday School classes, Whitney took one look at me and said, "Are you okay?"

I nodded. I told her I really liked the psalms of lament and that David "got me" when it came to my present feelings of anger and lamenting.

Whitney slowly nodded back and raised her eyebrows. She didn't say much then, but later told me she was a little worried about me that morning after that interaction. I think she was concerned that I wholeheartedly seemed to enjoy jumping on the bandwagon of furious God-lovers.

But it was a morning of music that began the process of a new understanding for me. I had known about the Psalms for years before that day. I could have told you that many of them were songs of lament and that David grew angry at God at times in his life. I probably would have even described David as an emotional man. He played the harp and wielded a mean slingshot against giants. He killed lions with his bare hands. He was definitely a creative type and therefore it seems logical that he was potentially moody as well.

But, it wasn't until I deeply lamented in my own soul that the Psalms ministered to me in a powerful way. They don't sugarcoat David's life or failures. That's one of the things I love most about God's Word, and it makes the Psalms even more rich and personal to me. Nobody is trying to hide anything or appear to have it all together.

David was not a perfect man. He committed some sins that are still considered the "big ones" in this day and age. He didn't always get it right. He sinned in his anger. But his anger was not always wrong. Sometimes his anger led him to redemption.

I wanted to be on that same path toward redemption. Not redemption in the sense of God saving my soul, because he had already finished that work on the cross, and I'd accepted it as a small child. No, now I desired the redemption of my present mess. Allowing God to take hold of my loss and pain and make beauty out of the ashes of my smoldering emotions. Redeeming, buying back, this loss for His glory, and ultimately, drawing me, his little child, into His loving arms. Because God's love, in the midst of the pain, and sin, and loss of this broken world, is what redemption is all about.

I didn't handle the loss of this baby in a perfect manner. Of course not! How could any sinner handle anything in a perfect manner?

My sense of entitlement, and feeling as if I'd deserved anything from God, was wrong. I won't say it was silly, but I will say it was sin. It's not a long journey between disappointment and entitlement. So, to find myself there was not surprising. Hormones and grief helped expedite the trip. But, I knew in my heart the wrongness of my attitude and that I deserve nothing. Everything is a gift from God. Everything. Every heartbeat, my own and that child's in my womb, is something I could never do enough, think enough, pray enough, wait enough to earn. It can't be earned. It is a gift.

My husband had spoken it to me first. I needed time, and God's intervention through an Australian band, to help me hear it.

It seems in marriage, sometimes words, like Kraig's insensitive comments about my finger injury turn out to be mistaken, and lend to joy and great teasing in proving the other wrong.

At other times, there's no delight involved in delivering the hard words. It's love, but love delivered through truth. Not the easy type of truth, like revealing that a knuckle is indeed fractured, but the painful truth of suggesting a heart may be out of line instead. Though it's difficult to hear such words through the dust and the noise, it is true love at its finest.

Our garage remained a mess, but the dust settled in our life, in general, as time put more days between the awful ultrasound and us.

My anger toward Kraig slowly faded. My love for him never wavered. If anything, it grew.

Anger still simmered, but not toward Kraig, or God either. Kraig had helped me work through it, and I was now working through it with God. I told God that I was still lacking the warm fuzzy feelings of His love. But, I knew without a doubt that He did love me. He would just have to continue to prove it over and over, as He has my entire life.

I did my part too. I chose to open my eyes and ears to a couple of realities. That sometimes, even when you don't feel God's love, you can see and hear it. And that love just may look a lot like a husband leaning on a broom.

*   *   *

As my body and soul healed, Kraig and I realized we hadn't finished our conversation about how many children we wanted. In fact, it was only beginning.

The miscarriage had opened quite a can of worms. Now friends and family knew we were not necessarily "done." Our children knew that adding another sibling to the family was within the realm of possibility, though especially the youngest two still had no idea how this came to be. Thankfully they weren't asking many questions, at least not ones we couldn't avoid with a simple, "Do you want a snack?" diversion.

But Kraig and I knew we couldn't avoid the topic for long. We continued to age and the only thing we knew for certain was that having another child would have to happen sooner rather than later.

So, we discussed it. And we discussed it. And then we discussed it some more.

We went over all of the facts. The ages of our children, our ages, our ages plus nine months, our ages plus eighteen years. Our bank statement. Our bank statement minus sending three kids to college and paying for two daughters' weddings. No, make that potentially four kids going to college and who knows, maybe another wedding. What about the loss of my potential income, which I didn't currently actually earn, but could if we didn't have another child and I started working when Kenzie went to school. So subtract that hypothetical potential unknown income from what I could earn if I were to go back to work five years earlier than if we did add another child. Better yet, let's subtract six years, depending on where the hypothetical child's birthday falls in the school calendar year.

Thus it went.

The math, and the logic, and the discussions, and the planning, and the dreaming, and the hoping, and the adding, and the subtracting, and the talking. The questions from the kids about another baby. The longings to hold a newborn in a onesie. The panic of aging bodies that would not operate well with interrupted sleep. The questions from friends and family about another baby. The thought of another voice heard around our dinner table. The thought of another mouth to feed. The desire to give our love to one more. The imagining of what he or she would look like. The suggestion of names. The occasional thought of feeling pretty crowded in the kitchen already.

All of this doesn't even bring into account the spiritual aspect of our discussions. Both of us deeply sought to do what God wanted for our family, and so we talked about Scripture, God's heart for children, God's plan for families, God's will, and the commentaries and sermons of pastors we respected.

All of the thinking and discussing just about killed us.

We were dying a slow death by discussion. The dead horse had been beaten to a pulp. The discussions occurred not over the course of a few dates, but during every single date. And not just dates, but we discussed it late at night after the kids went to bed when tiredness and irrational emotions had taken over and added to our confusion. We discussed it on long car trips, on the way home from church, during phone calls, and basically every time we could do so with minimal interruption between October 2013 and October 2015. Two years! Two years of these dragging-on, nail-biting, tear-evoking, mind-numbing, anger-inducing conversations.

Granted, we lived our lives as "usual" in most ways. We were struggling with this "slice of life," the slice of whether or not our family was complete, but not every piece of our "cake" was troubled. We were not constantly walking around in a funk, and most people would have had no idea this issue stymied us. It was a private conversation. A private struggle. There were also many areas of life where we found much joy and delight.

But, in this one area, we were stuck.

Stuck on the whether or not to add "Number Four."

*   *   *

Thirty-four

Originally posted on *Ten Blue Eyes* blog, March 24, 2012

Twenty-three years ago today, my mom, Mary Miller, died suddenly of a heart arrhythmia. She was thirty-four years old.

This Friday is my birthday. I will be turning thirty-four.

I'm going to be very honest here and admit that I'm struggling with turning thirty-four. It has nothing to do with aging, and I'm not one bit superstitious, so the number itself doesn't bother me. I guess what bothers me is the realization of how young my mom was when she passed away. This realization sits with me differently at age thirty-four than it did at age ten.

I always knew she died young. I also knew it was such a sad thing that she left my dad with two little children, ages ten (six days shy of eleven) and six. But now that I'm turning thirty-four, I see her death through a different lens. Now I'm not a child. I have children of my own. I see the loss of my mom through my own mommy eyes. And it has changed my perception.

My mommy eyes see things around my house now, like rubber darts stuck to light switches, and Barbies on the counter, and I realize that my own mom missed seeing a lot of things. She missed my middle-school years, my AAU basketball games, shopping for my prom dress, and planning my wedding.

She didn't get to see my dad walk me down the aisle toward the most wonderful man. Boy, she would have loved my husband!

And it's so sad that her grandchildren will never meet her this side of Heaven. It makes these mommy eyes cry at times.

But, as I've become one of those grown-ups who realizes how young thirty-four really is, I've wiped my eyes and often recalled a story my dad told me once about my mom. He told me that his beloved church secretary, who was like a mother to him, had passed away while my mom was still living. My dad had gone to visit her grave, depressed and grieving. He was having trouble moving past the grief. But he said that my mom looked at him and asked, "Why do you look for the living among the dead?" She was quoting Scripture. Luke 24:5 to be exact. It reads:

"On the first day of the week, very early in the morning, the women took the spices they had prepared and went to the tomb. They found the stone rolled away from the tomb, but when they entered, they did not find the body of the Lord Jesus. While they were wondering about this, suddenly two men in clothes that gleamed like lightning stood beside them. In their fright the women bowed down with their faces to the ground, but the men said to them, 'Why do you look for the living among the dead? He is not here; he has risen! Remember how he told you, while he was still with you in Galilee: "The Son of Man must be delivered over to the hands of sinners, be crucified and on the third day be raised again."' Then they remembered his words." (Luke 24:1-8)

I like how it says in the last verse that then they remembered his words. Before that they had been so caught up in their grief that they didn't remember Jesus' promises. The angels helped give them perspective and helped them look for a living God.

I know my mom is no longer living on this Earth, and she never will again. However, when I allow Christ to change my perspective, I can remember that she is living in Heaven. She is happy and whole. She didn't want my dad to be overcome with grief and lose perspective on life when he lost his secretary. I know that she most certainly wouldn't want me to sit and mope often for her.

Yes, I do sometimes mope, and there is no way to get around the fact that it's heartbreaking. She missed so much. Yet, I try to focus on what she did see and more importantly, *Who* she is seeing now.

It makes my mommy eyes sparkle along with the tears. It makes me want to embrace every day with my children and direct their eyes toward our loving and living Heavenly Father. I try to live by the motto, "Wherever you are, be all there." I don't know what my own future holds or what will come in my life but I want to enjoy this moment. Now. Today.

And when thinking about the future, I want to be like the woman described in Proverbs 31:25 who "is clothed with strength and dignity;" and "can laugh at the days to come." You'd think that after having such a hands-on education about God's provision and love in a worst-case scenario that I'd have graduated from this lesson already. But unfortunately I have to go over the notes again and again. God is living, active and unchanging. He has proven faithful in the worst, and He'll be faithful no matter what is to come. I study these thoughts often and feebly try to teach my own children these truths.

I miss my mom. I wish I could talk to her now. Mom to mom. Woman to woman. Instead I hear her echo the angel's words in my mind. "Why do you look for the living among the dead?" Live life today, Christy. Yes, do remember the sorrow, because God uses all things for the good of His people. In sorrow we grow so much in our faith, but don't stop there. Look to the Living God today. And live.

I am trying to look all around with those mommy eyes. I see pigtails, and peanut butter-stained fingers. I see toys and shoes and crumbs on the floor. I see smiles and innocent sweet little eyes on my children's faces. I see grace and blessings heaped upon the sorrow.

I see now.

And now I'm turning thirty-four.

* * *

Kraig and I were hearing the conflicting sounds of the second hand ticking and the heartstrings strumming. I could not let it go. I wanted a fourth child.

There was something about ending on a loss that I disliked. Remember how much I hate to lose? I wanted to keep trying. And we did.

We did not get pregnant.

Tick. Tock. Tick. Tock.

Kraig was becoming more and more adamant that he was feeling done. That our family was complete.

Back when the tables had been turned, and Kraig was willing to add another child and I was not, Kraig never pushed it. He never made it "a thing." He was simply willing and open, but not pushing those desires on me. However, now that I was the one wanting another child, and Kraig was leaning away from that desire, I made it an issue. I was not as gracious or patient as he had been. I was driven to get my way. To win.

When my body didn't cooperate by getting pregnant, my mind started to turn to another option. Adoption. This brought up an entirely new offshoot for our discussions. It only added to the heaviness and duration of each one. Could we adopt? Should we adopt? How would we adopt? We hashed out scenarios and went back to the bank statements and wrung our hands over it all.

My mind became overactive and its wheels spun in the adoption

143

rut. It consumed me. I was no longer stuck on our Christmas stocking holders spelling "Peace." I was ready to figure out how to add a sixth. Soon, I realized adoption was not only consuming my conscious thoughts, but that it was also consuming my dreams, and not just while I slept, but my daydreams as well.

I was driving to Indianapolis for a meeting for the foundation that supports the children's hospital that had treated Karson's leukemia. As I drove the two hours to Indianapolis for the all-day meeting, I daydreamed about crazy scenarios. Maybe there would be a baby in the hospital (which I wouldn't even be setting foot in that day anyway as our meetings were held in a local hotel conference room) that needed a family. Maybe the hospital foundation staff, with whom I was meeting, would ask if we wanted to adopt this imaginary yet up-for-adoption baby. Could I run to Target and buy an infant car seat for the drive home and maybe a few pairs of footy pajamas?

Before I realized it, I had mentally taken this child home and had introduced him to Kraig and the kids. I was planning out how to decorate his room. All the while, the green mile markers slowly passed by my passenger window in a car where I would remain the only occupant that day.

This wasn't the only time I found myself in such daydreams. It happened often. I had allowed this mental pattern and now unleashed, I could not catch it. It was running out of control.

I began to pray about adoption regularly, and of course I continued to talk to Kraig about it too. He repeatedly told me that he loved adoption, believed in it, and highly supported it, but did not personally feel called to it. I did not understand how he could feel this way.

"How could a child ever be wrong?" I questioned him.

Then we'd hash out the same paragraphs that we'd voiced the week before. The same dialogue was on repeat as if a needle was stuck on a vinyl record. The sound of our own voices grated on our ears.

Kraig would say that if I were going to use the argument that a child could never be the wrong answer, then I had to carry that logic out exponentially. "So if four kids is right, then five kids is too. And six kids, and seventeen. Are we going to have seventeen kids?"

I was pretty sure I didn't want seventeen kids.

But I did want four.

I didn't want to discuss this logic, I just wanted him to want what I wanted. One more kid. I felt like that was fair to ask and I didn't want to carry over any exponents or figure out what x equaled.

One night, in an effort to make our discussions more fruitful, instead of just bearing repeated discord, Kraig suggested I start exploring adoption options so we would know what exactly we were discussing. He said if I looked into cost, agencies, how long it would take, etc., then we would have more of an idea of what we were deciding.

(*Tick. Tock. Tick. Tock.*)

And I did. I researched and read. I continued to pray for wisdom and direction. My mind had been warming up for this moment, stretching its muscles and running in place. I was eager, ready, and thrilled to accept the task of learning practical next steps.

I found three main options that seemed viable.

First, I had several acquaintances who had gone through an organization that brought children with special medical needs to the United States for surgeries. One friend had a boy in her home for years, and he became a part of their family. I called her. I asked all about the cost and details and credibility of the organization. She patiently answered all my questions and issued a warning that the end goal of this program was not adoption, but to help these children with their medical needs, and then send them back to their homes and families who had already sacrificed valuable time to send them to the States. She told me that her situation with this young boy was very unusual. I greatly appreciated her insight and honesty. This was not the right direction for us. I was interested in learning more about adoption, not a short-term placement.

Next, I talked to a friend from college who has adopted five children herself and who was an advocate for a local adoption service. Again, I hit the jackpot of kindness and sincerity with the information she offered to me. This sweet friend even prayed with me and spent much time going over details and information. This option looked good, but we would have to start with training, and classes, and payments soon. The ball was in my court. All we needed to do was decide to go for it and things would start rolling.

The third option was a long shot, but I couldn't let it go without checking into it. As I thought about adoption, no particular country, domestic or foreign, plucked on my heartstrings. They all sounded fine, but none reverberated with a calling. But then I thought about a child with cancer. Now that hit home. My mercy and compassion for children with cancer had grown tremendously after our son's cancer journey. Yes, I wanted to find out if there was a way we could adopt a child with cancer.

I called the pediatric cancer clinic where our son still goes for annual checkups. The social worker there is a delight, and I consider her a friend. When she answered, I told her I was calling as a patient, but even more as a friend. I told her about our third miscarriage and how I still had the desire for another child. Then I asked her the big question, "Is there any chance we could adopt a child with cancer?"

She was so gracious in her reply, but explained that it was highly unlikely. She said even if a child was abandoned because of their medical needs, we'd need to be licensed foster care providers or have a home study and everything done to be legal and ready to adopt. Even with all of that in order, the chances of a child with cancer being available for adoption were slim to none. I understood.

I reported all of these findings to Kraig. His own desire to adopt was not stirred with the imparting of this additional information, yet he listened carefully. He told me he would adopt if I wanted to, but that he still did not feel called.

I hated that we weren't on the same page, but I proceeded nonetheless. It was foreign territory to head down a road without us both being passionate about the destination. Kraig said he'd go there, do this adoption thing, if I wanted to. And I did. So I decided we would. I chose the second option, the adoption agency my friend was involved in. She had explained to me how to get things moving, and I was ready to accelerate.

Kraig had better fasten his seat belt.

*   *   *

Victory! After two years of countless conversations, a decision had been made. I was elated! It was time to tell someone else about our decision. Though the topic had been such a hot one between Kraig and me over the previous twenty-four months, we had rarely spoken about it to anyone else. Not even our parents. A few of my girlfriends had heard my rambling thoughts and frustrations, and Kraig had talked to a few of his friends as well. But for the most part, it was not something we'd shared with others. We wanted it to be our discussion and decision. No one else's.

Now that we'd come to a decision, I was ready to spill the beans. I called my parents (my dad remarried and I call her "Mom") and asked if I could stop by in a few minutes and talk to them. They both happened to be home and agreed it was fine for me to stop over. I had at least an hour before needing to be at my son's school, where I was volunteering for one of his fifth grade activities, and I figured an hour would be plenty of time to deliver the news.

Mom and Dad were curious, I'm sure, as to why I suddenly wanted to talk. We sat in their living room and I started right in.

"Kraig and I have decided we're going to adopt." I smiled and drew in a deep breath.

My parents were delighted and smiled back. They asked several questions and listened.

But the following hour of conversation did not go as I had anticipated. And it wasn't my parents' voices that made it so. It was my own.

Because as I continued to share Kraig's and my plans and desires, I realized I was sharing *my* plans and desires. Kraig was a side note. A willing participant, yes, but more of an "extra" on the set than a key role player.

When the acceptance of what I already knew finally sunk in, it broke me.

I began to sob.

"Where are these emotions coming from?" my dad asked from his spot in his favorite recliner.

I continued to cry and struggled to talk though the tears. I told them I didn't really know. That maybe Kraig and I shouldn't do this after all because we weren't on the same page. It was me who wanted to adopt. It was me who trying to make it all happen. And it was me for whom Kraig was doing it.

My parents assured me that they knew Kraig and I wanted to make the right decision, and they had no doubt we would. They also said they'd pray with us and would share any wisdom they had, but they'd trust us to do what we felt was right.

I kept checking the clock on the wall and I knew I had to leave. I was due at Karson's school soon. Tears still wet my swollen face. My makeup smeared under my puffy eyes. I went into their restroom and tried to fix my disheveled face. My efforts were pointless. I didn't have time to go home and reapply my mascara. My eyes were so swollen anyway, it probably wouldn't have mattered.

I arrived at the school a few minutes late, but the teachers and other volunteers had saved me a spot. I was to help with an educational teambuilding game outside on the school lawn.

I had not worn a coat on this unusually cold fall day and the wind kept whipping me in the face. I just hoped the other adults thought my eyes were red because of the weather.

*   *   *

"This is a win-lose situation." I told Kraig. "One of us is going to get our way, and the other is not. The other is going to lose."

"I don't see it that way," Kraig said bluntly. He drew in a quick, sharp breath like he does when he's making a point, and it irritated me.

How could it not be that way? How could one of us not end up losing in this scenario when we both wanted opposite things?

I operated under this mindset for months. We did not feel a peace to move forward with adoption. We had not gotten pregnant. It seemed time was making the decision for us that we were not going to have a fourth child. I was losing.

Just as with a balloon volleyball game with my children in the living room, I don't like losing. I don't like it at all.

*   *   *

As much as I wanted to win, as the months rolled by, there was something I desired even more than winning. Peace. Like the stocking hangers on our mantel.

I wanted peace about the subject of "Number Four," as Kraig and I had now been calling it for almost three years. Peace not only eluded me now, but I did not see a future in which I'd ever find it regarding this topic.

My soul twisted inside me. It was wrung tight. I was dying a slow death by lack of a definite decision—and by a conversation topic that would not be put out of its own misery.

Kraig and I were feeling the strain on our marriage. Us. The couple who had prayed since their engagement that their marriage and home would be full of peace and joy. Now peace and joy seemed to have paired up and hidden from us like in a game of Sardines. We didn't like playing this game.

We set some new ground rules. On dates, which were precious commodities anyway and not to be wasted on more strife, we deliberately decided to have fun; we'd ban the "Number Four conversation" from the evening. We'd go to a movie, out to ice cream, a Mexican restaurant, somewhere we could relax and enjoy each other. We'd intentionally focus on other topics of conversation and we'd try hard to laugh and reconnect.

It helped a little. But, to mix metaphors, the elephant was still in the room nervously walking circles around the rancid corpse of a badly beaten horse. PETA was getting suspicious.

So, we tried a different approach. It looked like we'd have to remove the discussion all together, not just ban it on dates. And to remove it, we'd have to come to a definite answer. More than once we tried to "rip the Band-Aid off" the conversation by just saying it was over. We'd sit and discuss and conclude the following: Kraig was not called to adopt. He was willing to do so for me, and therefore, I felt very loved by him, but I also therefore did not feel a peace to move forward with adoption either. I knew we needed to be in it together. We had tried to get pregnant since the third miscarriage, and we had not. Time was marching on and Kraig was now in his forties. I was in my late thirties, and we were both growing more uncomfortable with the idea of a newborn the older we got.

So, we'd say it aloud. We're done. This conversation is closed.

We'd get down on our knees in front of our couch and we'd hold hands and pray together. We'd once again surrender it all to God, as we had many times before, and we'd tell Him we felt as if He was leading us to this conclusion, and we just wanted to be obedient.

Come out, come out wherever you are, Peace. We know you're around here somewhere. We've made a decision. We're done playing this game. It's over.

Peace?

Hello?

A few weeks or months later, we'd find ourselves having the same conversation. It kept coming back up. Like those trick birthday candles that you light and blow out and then they relight on their own. We kept blowing the conversation out, and it kept reigniting.

Each time we'd hash out the same conclusions. We'd agree together, and then in front of God on our knees by the couch. I'd cry every time. My tears would fall off of my cheeks and onto the brown suede material, a salt bath for the furniture.

We had made the decision with our minds, but our hearts had not yet caught up. Peace must have been waiting to arrive until our hearts were involved.

I couldn't will my heart to catch up, but I could help move it in that direction by living out the decision we'd made. Living during lamenting was becoming a repeated topic. I'd learned earlier, through the music and teaching of the Sons of Korah, that David lamented and lived. His lamenting was healthy in that he was not denying the pain or the problems, but he allowed them to lead him toward redemption of the circumstance. The lamenting and living realigned his heart with God's. It was a process, a lamenting and living cycle. A difficult practice.

Sometimes we obey even when we don't feel like it. That's part of training our hearts to align with God's. It takes the focus off of ourselves, and our own desires, and puts it back on God.

I have also learned that in order to get my emotions in check, as I lament and live, and truly change my heart, I must start with my mind. I asked God to help me reign in my thoughts so that I'd no longer daydream about adopting or being pregnant. Though it was tough, I retrained my thoughts to think about obedience and trust. To focus on the here and now and to count my blessings instead of my losses.

One of those blessings was the realization that my husband had been willing to engage in this conversation for so long. He could have shut it down months ago, but he did not. I was fairly certain many other men would not have had the patience Kraig had displayed. This patience was kindness to me. A gift. I found myself grateful for that, even if through gritted teeth.

*   *   *

Gratitude through Gritted Teeth

Originally posted on *Ten Blue Eyes* blog, November 22, 2016

I knew there was a fee to park at the venue where I was taking my two young daughters to the *Disney Princesses on Ice* show. But I forgot.

Not until I was driving in to the large lot did it dawn on me that I had no cash. And they don't accept credit cards for parking. I could not enter. Instead I was turned away and drove back onto the busy street. My daughters began to panic.

"Mommy! Isn't that where the Princesses are going to ice skate?"

"Why did you turn around, Mommy?"

I pulled into a retail parking lot and searched the van's cup holders for loose change. Not enough. I scavenged through my purse. I came up short. I did not have my ATM card on me, and by the time I drove home to get enough cash to park, we would miss most of the show for which my girls had been counting down the days.

I let out a deep sigh of frustration.

Then it hit me. I had friends who were also attending this show. Maybe they could meet me in this lot and let me borrow some money. I called. They were already in their seats at the show, but in an act of complete kindness, my friend's husband ran cash out to me near the front doors.

We made it! We settled into our seats just as the show was starting. The mesmerizing performance left my girls, ages six and four, with huge smiles and twinkling eyes as they watched the princesses twirl and jump. Just watching my girls gave me a huge grin.

It had taken me part of the first act to stop sweating and to settle in, but I had done so. I tried to take in each magical moment of making this memory with my daughters.

When the show ended, we walked down the long, concrete corridor winding our way out of the massive building. Hundreds of other people flowed along with us. Every ten feet or so, vendors were selling Disney merchandise. Princess dolls, toy swords, glowing sticks, and more. My girls begged for something. I hesitated, but gave in to the pressure as I again reasoned it was such a special evening.

The snow cones came in plastic souvenir princess cups. I forget the exact price, but it was somewhere near $10,000. Or maybe $10. Both felt outrageous. I bought two. I figured my girls' delight would last for weeks to come.

I was wrong.

As we continued to walk down the long hallway we passed more vendors.

"I really wanted a doll, Mommy!"

"Why won't you buy me a Princess dolly?" the little one whined.

The complaints continued. Didn't they know I had already spent a lot of money just on the tickets for this show, let alone the parking fiasco, which had left me indebted to my friends? Then, I had just bought them snow cones in a princess cup and I had about had enough of this giving spree to ungrateful little people.

A few more words of complaint came out of their mouths before I stopped. Dead in my tracks. I put my hands on their shoulders and walked against the flow of traffic until I squeezed the three of us into a corner. I backed the girls against a cold concrete wall.

"I am tired of this complaining. You have been given so much already. We are not moving until you guys are thankful!" I said in a huff.

I further stated my case. "I just spent a lot of money on tonight and instead of being thankful for it, you're complaining and asking for more. I've had it! You will stand there until you are thankful. Do you hear me?"

The girls nodded as their little lips, stained purple and red from their snow cones, began to quiver. They whimpered and cried as the crowd slowly moved by us.

There they were. Two little blonde girls standing against a wall trying to feel thankful.

(P.S. This was not my finest parenting moment.)

"Are you thankful yet?" My voice was firm. I demanded an answer.

They sniffed and cried and shook their heads. After a few more minutes I decided they were thankful enough and we continued on our way. I heard no more requests for princess dolls. Only sniffles.

Today, as I was doing dishes, two years after that evening, I picked up the souvenir princess cup off the counter and smiled.

"Are you thankful yet?" I laughed to myself.

I'm not proud of how I handled that moment, but I am thankful for it. Today as I thought back over the memory, I realized that I was trying to instill gratitude in my children. I was aiming to make thankfulness a habit for them, an automatic response. And I was trying to get out of there without going bankrupt. But mostly, I was teaching my kids to be grateful.

That's a hard lesson to learn.

I know how they felt that night. Sometimes I don't feel very thankful either. I get caught up in what I don't have instead of noticing all the blessings in front of me. Sometimes I need someone to stand me up against a cold wall until I get my wits about me and express the gratitude I don't feel.

Feeling grateful isn't necessary for being grateful.

Sometimes you say thanks through gritted teeth.

And, that's okay.

It's all part of the training.

*   *   *

I desperately wanted God to heal my emotional wounds. I asked Him to help restore Kraig's and my relationship to one of joy and peace— as we'd so often prayed it would be. I asked God to help Kraig and me feel peace in our own hearts. And, I prayed for God to confirm, deep in my soul, that the decision truly was in obedience to Him.

Then, one day while I was praying, I returned to lamenting. I cried out to my Father in complete transparent honesty. I told God how I just didn't understand why He would say a child was the wrong answer. How dare He? How could He, the one whom I believed created life itself, say another life was not the answer?

And then I knew. I knew deep in my heart.

It's not what I have for you.

I wish I heard it in a voice resembling Morgan Freeman's, or saw it written in the clouds. But I didn't. I just knew it. And actually, knowing it is even better than seeing it.

It's not what I have for you.

Having more children or adopting a child honors God and is dear to His heart. His plan for many, many people includes these things. He desires many to have four or more children. But it wasn't what He had for me.

There, I found peace.

I didn't have a reason, but I had an answer.

I had believed that because I was willing to make what I perceived as sacrifices to add another child to our family, like sleepless nights, difficult transition periods, potential sibling issues, and financial strain, that it must be what God desired from me. I had believed a myth that difficulty equaled God's will. But I never found that principle in the Bible. Sure, many times God's will is difficult. But He's not concerned with our comfort as much as He is with our obedience. We cannot detect God's will by the degree of difficulty involved.

We detect God's will by seeking His heart, and aligning our own with His.

I read Hosea 6:6. "For I desire mercy, not sacrifice, and acknowledgement of God rather than burnt offerings."

God was telling the disobedient people of Hosea's day that they had gotten it wrong. He wasn't looking for mere burnt offerings or sacrifices, He didn't want them to just go through the motions. He was looking at their hearts.

This shook me. When I aligned my heart with His, I realized another child was not a wrong or sinful thing at all. It was just not what God had for me.

Guess who else helped me understand this? Old Testament David. Him again! I seem to relate to his emotional highs and lows. I was comforted by his lamenting, but I've also been comforted by his living.

David possessed a desire in his heart much like the desire I had for another child. David wanted to build a temple for God in Jerusalem. Now, this seems like a noble idea. David's motive is right in this desire, from all we can tell. He wants to build a permanent structure for worship after all the years Israel has been wandering in the desert with only a tent for worship (the Tabernacle). Now, they are settled after many bloody war campaigns, David is king, and he wants to build a temple for God.

2 Samuel 7:1 reads, "After the king was settled in his palace and the Lord had given him rest from all his enemies around him, he said to Nathan the prophet, 'Here I am, living in a house of cedar, while the ark of God remains in a tent.'"

David desires a good thing, to build a temple for the worship and honor of God.

But, God says no.

Harsh?

When you're the one that God is telling no, yes, it sure *feels* harsh. It stings.

God tells David, through the prophet, Nathan, that his son will be the one to build the temple.

2 Samuel 7:12-13: "'When your days are over and you rest with your ancestors, I will raise up your offspring to succeed you, your own flesh and blood, and I will establish his kingdom. He is the one who will build a house for my Name, and I will establish the throne of his kingdom forever.'"

God told David no. David's kingship was marked by war. God chose to use Solomon, who would rule in a time of peace, to build the temple. (2 Chronicles 22:7-10) But God did throw some other really amazing promises in with his answer, such as allowing Jesus Himself to come from David's line. (2 Samuel 7:16)

God still cares and gives good things, even if it's not the thing we want so desperately. Yes, this is comforting to me, but there's more.

In two places in the Old Testament, 1 Kings 8, and 2 Chronicles 6, we see this story come to fruition. Solomon, David's son, does indeed build the temple, and in these passages, he dedicates it to God.

Solomon gives a speech, and a phrase in its midst feels like a hug to me. He says,

> My father David had it in his heart to build a temple for the Name of the Lord, the God of Israel. But the Lord said to my father David, "You did well to have it in your heart to build a temple for my Name. Nevertheless, you are not the one to build the temple, but your son, your own flesh and blood—he is the one who will build the temple for my Name." (1 Kings 8:17-19)

Did you catch that one part? "You did well to have it in your heart."

Yes. Listen again.

"You did well to have it in your heart."

Wow. God takes the time to let David know that it was good that he had such a desire, but it simply was not what God had planned for his life.

This phrase speaks to me deeply and resonates in my heart and soul with love and compassion. No candy heart reading, "Be Mine," or "U R So Sweet," could ever compare to the amazing love this verse conveys.

I had asked God to confirm, deep in my soul, that the decision to be made was truly in obedience to Him.

And He did.

Building a temple was not what God had for David, but God reminded David that he did well to have the desire in his heart. And God continued to display His amazing love and goodness throughout the course of David's life.

Having a fourth child was not what God had for me, but God reminded me that I did well to have the desire in my heart. And God continues to display His love and goodness throughout my days.

*   *   *

The incredible peace lifted an elephant's worth of weight off of my chest. Physically, my countenance improved. My lungs filled full of air again.

I had desperately wanted another child, and I had been angry at God for not allowing it to be so. Then I had been angry and at unrest because I didn't understand why. What's crazy is, I still didn't. I had no real explanation as to why we'd miscarried and why we weren't both led to adoption, and why we did not get pregnant again. But for the first time in years, it didn't matter. I knew peace anyway.

I consistently found comfort in the fact that it was just not what God had for me. Once I accepted that, everything was different. Better.

Ultimately, I trust God. I have for as long as I can remember. I truly trust Him even when I don't understand.

That's where the sweetest peace is found.

Kraig was right. It wasn't a win-lose situation. There wasn't a winner, and there wasn't a loser. We both had struggled through this decision together and through it, though we weren't always on the same page, our love was "tested," and came out stronger for it. In a way, that made us both win.

I realize now that Kraig was showing me such great love in his response. He was willing to do something that he would not have otherwise chosen. He was willing to choose it out of his love for me. And that, my friends, is true love.

Though I did not get what I originally wanted, I did not lose. I gained. I gained a peace that passes all understanding. And a deeper understanding of how much my husband loves me. And how much my God loves me too.

Those are most worthy prizes.

*   *   *

In April of 2017, my first book, *Brownie Crumbs and Other Life Morsels*, was released. That day, my parents and my grandparents asked if they could take me to lunch to celebrate. I joked that I had a book launch team, and a book lunch team. Both were much appreciated.

We went to a local Italian place, and enjoyed sharing stories over our pasta. It was a special time of celebration. Afterward, as we walked to our cars, my parents helped my grandparents get into their car, and then they walked behind me to mine. As we parted ways, Dad said one last thing.

"I know how much you wanted another child, Christy. I can't help but think that this book is, in a way, like your fourth child. Something you brought into the world that probably wouldn't have happened if you would have had another baby or adopted."

I nodded. It was one of those times when I knew if I opened my mouth to respond, the floodgates would open. I'd cry. So I stuck with the nod and a smile.

I agreed.

I had not wanted my "fourth child" to look like a book. I had wanted an actual, squishy baby instead. They are much more of a delight to snuggle close and kiss. Instead, God made a way for me to write and release a book about my life, and it opened doors in the following two years to travel and speak to about fifty groups about hope, and faith, and His love.

Many times, as a way of introduction about myself, I'd tell the audience that I was married and had three children. Then, after elaborating a bit, I'd say that I felt as if my fourth child had been born on April 25, 2017, and it was a 12.2-ounce, six-by-nine inch book. This would bring a chuckle from the crowd and a natural transition into the heart of my talk.

God has used the book for His glory. I can't deny that and for it, I'm extremely grateful.

The three-year gestation for the book was a doozy. Here I thought nine months was long! But, the timing of the season, and the opportunity to release *Brownie Crumbs* was a gift. And a reminder that God can do things in answer to our prayers that are beyond our imagination and comprehension. Sometimes beyond what we even think we want too. But that's okay.

Because what I want most of all is to honor Him who makes it all possible.

*   *   *

This blog entry has been placed here, in the Lamenting and Living chapter, because it reminds me that we never know who our lives will touch, or how we'll leave an impact, just by simply living.

Letters from My Mother
Originally posted on *Ten Blue Eyes* blog, July 6, 2012

It was a dark and stormy night. It may sound frightening, but the scene wasn't something you'd see in a horror film. Instead it was just me, in my pajamas, sitting in a hotel breakfast nook with a cup of hot tea. I sat at a small round table with a large stack of letters. My family members all slept down the hall and the hotel lobby was quiet with just the occasional guest trickling in the front door. I could see lightning flashes out the nearby window but I didn't hear the thunder, or much of anything for that matter. I was focused. I was reading letters from my mother.

My grandmother, my late mother's mother, moved into a small apartment from her large eight-room farm house. During the packing and sorting that moving entails, boxes of letters were found. My mother and her two sisters had written home to their parents over the years (often once a week!) and my grandmother had kept the letters. Now I was holding a stack of these very letters that were written by my mother to her mother, some over thirty years ago.

My tired eyes scanned the worn pages back and forth as I gently unfolded each precious letter and looked closely at the postmark on the envelope. The letters in my stack started in 1976 when the postage stamp cost just thirteen cents. There was also a handwritten date on the front of each envelope that was put there by my grandmother to signify what day she mailed her reply to each letter.

Though I was tired from a long drive and a busy day of visiting with family and touring my grandmother's new apartment, I could not stop reading. I had been given an amazing gift. An opportunity to read my mother's own words about events that occurred before I was born. And as interesting as all of those details were, the best part was when I got to 1977-1978 and was able to read about her pregnancy with me, and the first year of my life.

Since her passing I've grown up and become a mother myself. I've often wished I could talk to her about her pregnancies and what I was like as a baby. But now I could read my mother's words.

I smiled as I read her accounts of morning sickness in the early stages of her pregnancy with me. She wrote to her own mother about her new personal record of vomiting seven times in one day. Who would have thought reading about throwing up could bring such pleasure! I laughed as I read that my parents thought I was going to be a boy based on my heart rate at a doctor's appointment. They even had a boy name picked out for me, Douglas Ray. It was never used, even when my brother was born.

I related when I read about the weeks after my birth when she wrote to her mother about her own tiredness and difficulty getting her tummy to look flat again. I chuckled at her cute sense of humor as she suggested that maybe the caramel sundae she just ate may be to blame for her lack of lost pounds.

As I finished my cup of tea and did my best to stay awake late into the night, I was continually touched. I was touched by my mother's love for her husband, my dad, and I enjoyed reading about their young relationship and her support of his growing ministry. I was moved to read about her anticipation of adding me to their family and overjoyed at her description of loving being a mother. My throat tightened and eyes stung a bit when I read statements like, "Christy can melt the hardest of hearts." Wow. She never could have known when she wrote those words just how much they would mean to her baby girl over three decades later.

When I finally gave in to my sleepiness and went to bed I was exhausted yet recharged. I was encouraged to remember to write things down for my own children, whether I'm around when they are grown or not. It's a gift to be able to read about your parent's life when they were in a life stage similar to your own. And when memories fail, these written details succeed in telling the story.

Some letters were handwritten and others were typed on a typewriter. All of them rang with my mother's voice and her sweet, funny and wise personality shone through the pages. They are a gift. They are letters from my mother.

*   *   *

Slice of Hope: Don't look for the living among the dead. Lament and live while remembering the eternal hope Christ brings through redemption. Don't strive for God's peace and love; accept them daily.

seven

change
and
new seasons

We sat on the Starbucks patio one summer evening. A group of ladies from a church in northern Indiana was interested in having me speak at their retreat later that fall. I loved that they took the time to meet me face-to-face first (because they were fairly local to my hometown), and to ask me some very direct questions about my beliefs before officially offering me the gig.

Once both parties were confident it would be a good fit, they told me the topic I'd be asked to speak about for the retreat, "Seasons of Change." I didn't tell them right then and there, but I almost instantly disqualified myself based on this topic. Handling change is not something I have mastered. In fact, I'm not even sure I'm getting a passing grade.

I did accept the speaking opportunity, and I did eventually tell them all my initial response. But, I also made sure to explain to the group that I would not be sharing about change that weekend from an expert's perspective, but from that of one who is in the daily struggle with them. I was one of them. Someone who wrestled with change, and therefore, I cared deeply about learning and sharing about ways to handle it better.

I was given three sessions to lead that weekend, and therefore, I decided to break the topic of change down into three types of change, and to try and tackle each one in its own respective session. The three types of change I chose were Catastrophic Change, Chronological Change, and Chosen Change.

I described them as follows: Catastrophic Change is something unexpected that occurs in your life that is usually negative, for example, the death of a loved one, an injury, the loss of a job.

Chronological Change occurs naturally due to the passage of time, like children going to kindergarten, becoming an empty nester, your own personal aging, the aging of your parents.

Finally, Chosen Change is an executed and often positive event, for example, getting married, starting a family, moving, starting a new career.

But as you know, change is change is change. There may be different types, but many of us struggle with change, and specifically, with the transitions into new seasons brought on by change.

It has been helpful for me to think of change in its "type" and to have some tools in my back pocket to combat any issues of difficulty I may have with that type of change. Let me share some things I've learned with you, but keep in mind, I'm still in the process of learning these tricks. I'm striving to apply these thoughts and ideas to more than these pages. I want them to become habits in my daily life.

Let's start with Catastrophic Change. We've all dealt with Catastrophic Change. Catastrophic Change can be clearly traumatic. Many of us have dealt with severe changes. Maybe it was the loss of a lifelong dream you held. Maybe others cannot see the catastrophe as you can see it, but to you, it feels big and it's a definite loss. Maybe it's living a life you didn't quite expect, and you're not sure you are happy with your present circumstances. Maybe you just have a general attitude of apathy and sadness toward life and that's not how you expected to live. All of these feelings can be brought on by Catastrophic Change, whether something occurred out-of-the-blue to make it so, or it was a gradual process with a sudden realization.

No matter how we got there, Catastrophic Change is no fun. It causes us to feel as if we're careening in a downward spiral.

My tools for dealing with Catastrophic Change sound a little trite when I say them together. Trust and adjust. I can't help the fact that they rhyme.

Trust. It sounds like I'm throwing a "church word" in your face, and I am. But let me tell you. If you truly believe in God, If you truly believe He is who He says He is, then you know He is sovereign over all. If you believe He's sovereign over all, then the next step to that belief would be to employ trust. For some reason, many of us stop with the belief and don't ever pull the ripcord on the trust parachute. We're heading toward the ground at a break-neck pace and the tool to help slow us down is within reach. Just pull the stinkin' cord! Utilize trust.

If we believe God is sovereign over all of life, then that includes Him being sovereign over change. Once again, I look to Scripture and see that when change is involved in the lives of the men and women we read about in the Bible, they are then required to still get on with life while either trusting in God to provide and sustain, or not trusting in Him. There isn't a third option in this one.

Let me add, that trusting has little to do with emotion. In fact, I'd say it's more about an action.

If you say you trust in a chair to hold your weight, you sit. You don't stand there and feel an overwhelming flood of emotion in your trust for the chair. You sit.

If you say you trust an Uber driver to get you to your destination, you get in the car. You don't stand there and allow your emotions to rule as you look at said Uber driver with great trust and admiration. That would just be weird. Get in the car.

If you say you trust God, even when things are going rough for you, then you trust by taking the next step. Doing the next thing in front of you, whether you do it robotically, or with great gusto, you do it. You move forward. You continue. You proceed.

You pull the ripcord on trust, and you regain some purpose in where you will land as you continue your journey.

*   *   *

Jeremiah 29:11: The Rest of the Story
Originally posted on *Ten Blue Eyes* blog, November 2, 2015

Perched on the top bunk of my third-story dorm room I had a good view of my fellow college students on the sidewalk below. I watched them pass as if staring at the second hand of a clock, absentmindedly watching the rhythm of the afternoon. I adjusted the pillow behind my back and leaned against the painted cinder block wall. My legs were folded under me, and my Bible lay open on my lap to Jeremiah 29. I wanted to know more about the plans God had for me.

As a sophomore on a Christian college campus, I had heard the words of Jeremiah 29:11 many times in reference to God's will for my future.

"'For I know the plans I have for you,' declares the Lord, 'plans to prosper you and not to harm you, plans to give you hope and a future.'"

Those words robotically came from the mouths of professors, chapel speakers, and friends as if someone had pulled a string on their backs that triggered a preloaded response whenever a question about the future arose.

I did not doubt that God loved me or had good plans for me, but as I struggled through worry about the unknowns of my future:

What degree should I work toward?

Who will hire me after graduation?

What type of job do I want?

Who will I marry?

Where will we live?

What type of job will my husband have?

I was looking for more than a pat answer. I was looking for peace in the midst of uncertainty. Jeremiah 29:11 seemed to be the go-to verse.

I wanted to know more about this apparent feel-good promise, so I read the context of the verse in its chapter, Jeremiah 29.

Confusion struck me.

The good feelings associated with plans for prosperity and hope were put aside. The verses leading up to verse eleven were not filled with smiles and sunshine. Jeremiah was speaking to Israelites who had been carried off, essentially as prisoners of war, to the country of Babylon.

The first verse of the chapter reads,

"This is the text of the letter that the prophet Jeremiah sent from Jerusalem to the surviving elders among the exiles and to the priests, the prophets and all the other people Nebuchadnezzar had carried into exile from Jerusalem to Babylon."

The fact that the word "surviving" is in this sentence tips me off that this was sent during a difficult time of war and death.

Jeremiah goes on to tell the people that they will one day be brought back to their homeland, Israel. God does have good things in store for them. He has plans to rescue them ... in seventy years. He knows His plans to help them.

Jeremiah 29:10-11 says, "This is what the Lord says: "When seventy years are completed for Babylon, I will come to you and fulfill my good promise to bring you back to this place. For I know the plans I have for you," declares the Lord, "plans to prosper you and not to harm you, plans to give you hope and a future."

I realized right then and there that verse eleven had been grossly taken out of context.

Not that God doesn't have plans for us ... not that God isn't a good God ... but God doesn't promise *me* anything in this passage. He was talking to Israelite POWs in Babylon!

What does this mean for my future? Does God still have plans and hope for me?

I squirmed on my plaid comforter and readjusted both my physical and spiritual position.

If Jeremiah 29:11 wasn't written to me, then why do we have it in our Bibles? Why read it at all? How can I know what is true for me and not just a message to its original audience?

To answer my complicated questions I go back to the simplest basics.

I believe God is who He says He is. I believe He is all-knowing and sovereign over all. I believe He never changes. Therefore, I can trust that any principle that I can glean about God from any passage of Scripture is still true today.

The specific promise of Jeremiah 29:11 wasn't written for me, but the principle that God was teaching the Israelites in that passage has not changed.

So what was the principle God was teaching His people?

I assumed from the way Christians had been quoting Jeremiah 29:11 that God was telling His people He was ready to swoop in and drop good things on those who loved and obeyed Him. That He was basically our Santa Claus with prosperity and hope in his sleigh. But the truth was, God wasn't going to deliver good things to His people the day that Jeremiah's letter was read to them, or even once a year under the tree, for that matter.

He was not planning to rescue them for seventy years.

And what really struck me were God's instructions for His people during those seven decades of *waiting*.

God told them to get on with life.

Jeremiah 29:4-8 reads:

"This is what the Lord Almighty, the God of Israel, says to all those I carried into exile from Jerusalem to Babylon: 'Build houses and settle down; plant gardens and eat what they produce. Marry and have sons and daughters; find wives for your sons and give your daughters in marriage, so that they too may have sons and daughters. Increase in number there; do not decrease. Also, seek the peace and prosperity of the city to which I have carried you into exile. Pray to the Lord for it, because if it prospers, you too will prosper.'"

The principle I learn here is that God *does* know the plans He has for us. He *does* have good things in store for our future. But while we are waiting, we are to live life and seek peace and prosperity, even if we're in enemy territory.

Wow.

I now see how I can relate and what I can learn from God's Word to His people. I'm not so different from the exiled Israelites after all.

I live in enemy territory because I live in this world. One day I know God will rescue me and will take me back to my homeland to dwell with Him. But the principle I learn from Jeremiah 29 is that while I'm here, I need to live. I need to seek the peace and prosperity of this place I call home for now.

I need to get to work because if the work of my hands prospers, God will prosper me too.

It sounds like this principle in Jeremiah 29 isn't all about what God has in store for me, but also how I can live for Him.

Jeremiah 29:11 is still a great verse to read for encouragement and hope. God hasn't changed since the days of Jeremiah. He knows the plans He has for me, and when they include bringing me home to be with Him, I know for a fact they are good.

But there's more to the story. God asks me to seek prosperity and peace in this territory while I wait for His rescue.

It looks like I had better get to work.

*   *   *

Once we begin to act on our trust during seasons of Catastrophic Change, we have to utilize the second tool in our toolbox (or back pocket, wherever you carry it.) Adjust.

I don't know about you, but I rarely get everything right the first time around. In fact, when people do get things perfect on the first attempt, we don't believe them. Remember the guy who bid the correct exact amount, down to the dollar, on his *The Price Is Right* showcase in September of 2008? He was scrutinized on the radio, television, newspapers, Internet, and around dinner tables from coast to coast. We don't actually expect perfection in most things, and so you'd think we'd be pros at adjusting. But we're not. I guess we're still trying to give ourselves permission to adjust.

When I have faced Catastrophic Change, like when our son was diagnosed with cancer, it took us awhile to adjust. People kept using the term "new normal" for our new cancer life, and new normal wasn't somewhere we arrived quickly after diagnosis. It took us awhile to find it. (I must have been using the GPS.)

It is okay to take time to adjust to life in general after a season of Catastrophic Change. You are probably going to fail to get it right for awhile. You may pull the ripcord on trust, you may move forward and live, but you may mess up. You may fall apart one day in your office and lay your head on your desk, sobbing. That's okay. Cry away. Then, wipe your tears and blow your nose. Adjust.

You may lash out in anger toward someone you love, or even toward a perfect stranger, and say something you regret deeply. That's okay. Apologize to them. Maybe give them a hug. Adjust.

You may be so caught up your Catastrophic Change grief that your mind can not focus on common everyday tasks. That's okay. Put your shoes on. Brush your teeth. One thing at a time. One step at a time. One breath at a time. Adjust.

*   *   *

That's How We Roll

Originally posted on *Ten Blue Eyes* blog, August 26, 2017

The grass squished damp and cold under me. The late summer sun was setting and the warm day gave way to a crisp evening. I wasn't prepared. My jacket remained in the car. I guess I'd need to adjust my thinking now that fall was fast approaching.

It's jacket season, Christy. Like it, or not.

I turned and looked over my left shoulder. My kids were standing on a small hill. Each had a golf putter in hand and a pile of golf balls at their feet. They were playing around on the putting green and I was enjoying the show. Mostly, I liked the commentary.

"Which of those three flags on the putting green are you aiming for?" I asked.

My middle child, the one who just turned nine, answered quickly.

"Whichever one the ball rolls closest to when I hit it."

I smiled and shrugged my cold shoulders. I guess sometimes we all adjust. Our mindsets, our golf swings, our wardrobes.

Earlier in the week, that same child sat and sobbed at the thought of making a decision. It wasn't even a bad set of options she was choosing between; fear overwhelmed her that she'd pick the wrong one.

"There is no wrong answer here, Karly," my husband said. "These are both good choices. Mommy and I understand that it's sometimes hard to make a decision, but what we have learned to do is to just pick one—to the best of our knowledge, and then later, if we need to adjust, we do." I stood there nodding my head in agreement.

Sometimes we just have to swing the putter, hit the ball, and watch where it rolls.

And then we adjust.

We learn. We think about how we hit the ball and what it felt like, and we decide if that's how we want to do it again. Or, do we want to try something different next time? Should we try to aim at something else?

Life is full of adjustments. Full of surprises. Confusion. Change. Clarifications.

That's okay. We truly live and learn every. Single. Day.

Sometimes we guide our decisions, and other times our decisions guide us.

Either way, we'll never be successful if we don't swing the putter, hit the ball, and watch it roll.

*   *   *

As much as I dislike Catastrophic Change, I loathe Chronological Change too. Chronological Change is the one that steals my precious toddler's baby fat, gives me "aging adult fat" in places I never had to worry about before, and takes my breath away as I look at old photos or videos that remind me of how much life has changed throughout the years.

I've always been nostalgic by nature, and I deal with Chronological Change quite frequently. Years ago, my friend, Stephanie, gave me a book by Karen Kingsbury called *Let Me Hold You Longer*. She'd chosen a thoughtful gift because we'd both just had sons one month apart. The book talks about recognizing not only the "firsts" of your children as they grow, but also the "lasts." The last time they'll reach for your hand to hold in public. The last time they'll crawl up on your lap. The last time they'll call you "Mommy" instead of "Mom." Oh my! It's making me sad to even think about these things. I'm such a savorer of life and moments, that sometimes I savor so hard it hurts.

I won't be surprised if my gravestone reads, "Here lies Christy Cabe. She savored the moment a little too hard and it finally did her in." I often wish I could slow down the hands of time, or stop it completely.

But time will not pause for me to catch my breath. It marches on, they say.

And so the tools I'm learning to use with Chronological Change are "See" and "Sow." This is not to be confused with a Seesaw. That's a different thing used for ups and downs in life.

First, "See" helps me to embrace the changes brought on by the passage of time by truly seeing what is in front of me. It's not going to take away every pain and twinge of sadness as life moves on faster than I prefer, but it does help.

Seeing the present helps us to savor what's in front of our faces before it's gone.

I am easily distracted. Sitting on the metal bleachers at my son's baseball game, I realize the scoreboard reflects a change has occurred in the game. A run scored, a strike was thrown. But I missed it. How? Maybe I was watching the lady in the lawn chair by the fence. Thinking about how cute her hair is today, and I like her sandals. Maybe my daughters ran up to me squealing in delight as they show off the string of dandelions they've tied together that stretch between them like a droopy finish line. Maybe I'm staring at my hands in my lap and am deep in thought about what a friend said to me in the school workroom earlier that day as we shared the paper cutter.

By the time I've turned my attention back to the game, I've missed some action. We all do it. But what else are we missing?

In my everyday life, I sometimes miss a moment because I'm looking at my phone, or am caught up in my thoughts. I may be looking at my daughter as she says, "Watch this cartwheel, Mom!" but I'm not truly seeing her.

We can't See everything. It is impossible. But, we can open our eyes to what is right in front of us. We can strive to do better. We can train ourselves to See more today than we did yesterday. Maybe tomorrow our eyes and minds will be yet a little less distracted.

We can put our phones down more often. We can push the power button on the remote and then push the preschooler in the swing. We can lay the book down (yes, even this one!) and look up at the world beyond the words on a page.

As a Little League coach tenderly puts his finger under the chin of the sobbing child who just made a crucial mistake, our focus also can be redirected. He steers his player's little wet eyes to his own and shows him that he's not angry. There's more to life than a scoreboard. Chin up. Look up. See more than the sadness.

Feel the finger under your chin today. Redirect your sight. You don't have to look far or wide. Just straight ahead.

*   *   *

See Now

Originally posted on *Ten Blue Eyes* blog, December 17, 2016

Why do I have to use the scissors to cut the tape off this dispenser? It's designed to tear off easily on these little pointy things. Annoying.

Should I wrap these gifts in one box or separate them so he has two presents to open?

Where did I put the scissors? How do I always manage to lose them?

"Mom!" my son yelled, his eyebrows raised and his tone firm.

"What?" I said shaken from my mental dialogue.

"I asked you three times what to put on this cut."

"What cut?" I asked.

"What do you mean what cut? I just told you! I have a cut on my foot and you said 'You do?' and then I asked if I should put a Band-Aid on it and you said 'Yes.'"

"I did?" This was not ringing a bell. How long had Karson been sitting there?

He continued, "Then I asked you if I should put anything on my cut before the Band-Aid and you're not answering me anymore."

My hands ceased moving. I lamely held the tape dispenser, feeling a bit dysfunctional. I willed my mind to catch up with the present.

"I'm sorry, Buddy. Even though I was answering you, I wasn't really listening. Now, let me see your foot."

It's not the only incident of multi-tasking malfunction I've experienced this holiday season. Unfortunately, my distracted and poorly executed interactions are piling up faster than gifts under my tree.

I swerved right into a retail parking lot from the left lane because the conversation on my phone was trumping my defensive driving skills.

I unloaded groceries from the trunk only to realize I forgot the one thing I went to purchase.

I clicked off the computer tab of a work project to open Amazon to shop for gifts that catch my eye.

I'm distracted in the present.

And when I see pictures from Christmases past my heart hurts as I realize how quickly chubby toddler cheeks have given way to little girl faces. How gifts of blocks and rocking horses have changed to those of video games and craft supplies. Ornaments with globs of dried glue and too much glitter remind me of sweet little hands that now color inside the lines.

The present will soon be the past.

I don't want to miss life in the future as it plays out in front of my face.

I want to appreciate moments as they happen.

I want to live in the now.

To stop my train of thought and still my hands.

To look. To see. To notice.

To pause my typing fingers and wink at my youngest child and study the way her whole face squishes up in such an adorable way as she tries to wink in return.

To look my oldest in the eye and laugh with him as he recounts the antics of the boys at his lunch table.

To hold my second grader's hand as we walk to the mailbox and to remember how soft her mitten feels in my cold, bare hand.

To feel. To smell. To taste.

To watch. To laugh. To hold.

To notice the now.

To see the present as the gift it truly is.

*   *   *

The other tool that helps with Chronological Change is to Sow. I'm not talking about using a needle and thread here, but a little faithfulness, obedience, eternal perspective, and elbow grease.

The fact is, time is going to move forward. We cannot stop it. One interesting thing about time? God is not bound by it. He calls Himself, "I Am" (Exodus 3:14), not "I Was" or "I Will Be." God is always in the present and always has been.

But, God being unbound by time does not stop Him from giving us "helps" as we live on Earth, stuck in time's grip. For one, God created time itself. Genesis 1 tells us He created all things in six days (He rested the seventh day). On the fourth day, he created tools for us to help mark time. Genesis 1:14 reads, "And God said, "Let there be lights in the vault of the sky to separate the day from the night, and let them serve as signs to mark sacred times, and days and years,".

God is the one who gave us days, years, seasons. Those things help us tremendously in the cycle of life. If we didn't have days, how would we know where to put our dentist appointments on the calendar? If we didn't have years, how would know when to throw that surprise birthday party?

"How old are you, anyway?"

"I have no idea."

If we didn't have seasons, how would we know when it was time to plant the seeds in the garden, or to watch the World Series instead of March Madness?

God has provided us a great gift by giving us time. He has given us a framework on which to operate. Slowing or stopping time would be messing with God's perfect framework.

Time and seasons are mentioned frequently in the Bible. There are obviously weather-related seasons, but there are also seasons for sowing, and weeding, and reaping. I could further explain, but Solomon already has. He wrote a popular passage about time and seasons in Ecclesiastes 3:1-8. It reads,

> There is a time for everything, and a season for every activity under the heavens: a time to be born and a time to die, a time to plant and a time to uproot, a time to kill and a time to heal, a time to tear down and a time to build, a time to weep and a time to laugh, a time to mourn and a time to dance, a time to scatter stones and a time to gather them, a time to embrace and a time to refrain from embracing, a time to search and a time to give up, a time to keep and a time to throw away, a time to tear and a time to mend, a time to be silent and a time to speak, a time to love and a time to hate, a time for war and a time for peace.

Time is for our benefit, and seasons aid us in our rhythm and purpose for life.

So, when I feel sadness due to the passage of time, I can sow. I can sow in two places, my mind, and my fields.

In my mind, I can sow reminders about God and time. Specifically, sow an eternal perspective, and the truth that God gave us time and seasons for our benefit. Maybe I've sowed these thoughts before, but I've forgotten them, or need to call them to mind again. Goodness knows you can have a good thought now and then and before you know it, it's gone. You have to practice sowing as a habit. Sow again. The good thought and attitude you sowed yesterday was drowned out by your to-do list, song lyrics from the 1990s, and your wifi password. Sow again.

As you struggle with Chronological Time, sow in your mind an eternal perspective. God has a bigger plan and purpose than the calendar on my fridge reflects. Even if I stacked all of the calendars for all of my years into a pile, they are only a drop in the bucket of God's ocean of purpose and plan. So remember, when you feel sad due to the passage of time, know it may be leading to a greater place and purpose.

You can also sow the reminder that God is the one who gave us time as a gift by creating days, and years, and seasons. The transition of seasons sometimes brings effort and discomfort. The tree must drop its leaves. The bulb must push its new stem through the dirt. The squirrel must bury his acorns. It takes effort to move into a new season, and a little bit of preparation and letting go of the last season. But God created it as so. The seasons are a gift. They are a good and natural part of His creation. Sow this reminder often.

If you need biblical encouragement for why you should sow in your mind, and not just my voice telling you to do so, you can listen to Paul. It's okay, I understand. I look for biblical backup of advice authors give me too. That is a good practice!

Paul says in 2 Corinthians 10:5, "We demolish arguments and every pretension that sets itself up against the knowledge of God, and we take captive every thought to make it obedient to Christ."

In this passage, Paul is telling the Corinthians how we (Christians) do not live by the standards of the world, but live differently, and he mentions involving our thoughts and minds.

Paul also talks about the mind with the Romans. He says in Romans 8:5-6, "Those who live according to the flesh have their minds set on what the flesh desires; but those who live in accordance with the Spirit have their minds set on what the Spirit desires. The mind governed by the flesh is death, but the mind governed by the Spirit is life and peace."

Life and peace, folks. That sounds pretty good.

I'll give you one more. This is encouragement from another biblical writer, Isaiah. Isaiah 26:3 says, "You will keep in perfect peace those whose minds are steadfast, because they trust in you."

Ah. Perfect peace. This is really sounding wonderful. It looks like the mind is a great place to start sowing.

Now it's time to sow your fields. Plant something in the world. Get to work. The fact is, our clocks are ticking. We will die someday. Our time is limited. So let's not waste it. You were placed on this Earth right now. This is your time. Sow your fields.

For me, in this season, sowing my fields is taking place in two main plots of land. One field looks like loving and being present with my husband and children on a consistent daily basis. They are my first priority. My most sacred ground. But, I am also called to write and speak about hope and faith. I love the work and toil those opportunities bring me too.

Sowing the field with my family sometimes yields great fruit. At the parent-teacher conference table, our daughter's teacher tells us our girl shows kindness to everyone in her class, regardless of how others treat those students. The teacher goes on to say she would want her own daughter to be like ours. This is a green and healthy sprout. The sowing of teaching Karly to show kindness to others has taken to the soil.

My son comes up behind me as I stand at the sink scrubbing a pot and he puts his long arm around my shoulders and says, "Thanks for doing laundry and dishes and taking care of us, Mom." I am stunned and silent as I taste the sweetness of this fruit. We sow the practice of gratitude and kindness in our home. And sometimes, though it's most difficult to show these things to the ones closest to you, the seedlings grow and thrive.

My husband pulls me close and whispers, "I'd marry you all over again. I waited until I was twenty-nine years old to get married because no one else was right for me. You are perfect for me. You're my favorite. I love you." The seeds we sowed in singleness of waiting and praying for the one God had for us have yielded an abundant crop of love.

But sometimes I teach my children to be kind and they lash out. Sometimes I do dishes for months without at single shoulder squeeze. Sometimes Kraig and I forget to speak our love into the other's ear. The sowing is happening, but the fruit isn't visible.

Sowing in my writing and speaking field sometimes looks really exciting, when books launch, and when I get to board a plane to fly across the country to share hope with a room of 500 women. These are low-hanging, plump pieces of fruit. Delicious. But they are the exception.

The common sowing in my writing and speaking field looks like me sitting in a chair, hands on the keyboard. There is typing, and deleting, and editing and head shaking. There are breaks I take to grab a cup of coffee, or workout and shower. Sometimes the words I've written sprout and grow and are used in the lives of others to grow fruit. Other times they die on my hard drive.

Sow anyway.

How do you do this? Ask yourself what you are feeling led to do with this season of your life. Is it starting a ministry to widows and orphans? That sounds pretty amazing! If so, start applying for a 501c3. Become a nonprofit. Sow your fields.

But, it doesn't have to be something so grand. Maybe your dream is to take time each evening to read the Bible to your children and to pray with them before you tuck them in. Great! Start this evening. It doesn't have to be an in-depth Bible study. Read them one verse. Say a short prayer. Sow your fields!

Maybe you've been toying with the idea of taking a photography class at the local community college so that you can be better equipped to use your camera to help with your friend's boutique business? Sign up. Snap away! Sow your fields.

Maybe you know soccer, or ballet, or baseball, and you could use your evenings coaching children. Batter up! Sow your fields.

Maybe you have a heart for the elderly, and you want to volunteer at your local nursing home. Maybe you want to sing on the worship team at church, or hold babies in the nursery, or lead a small group of teens. Maybe you feel called to bring encouragement to that girl you see at the gym each Wednesday.

I don't know specifically what your sowing looks like. But I do know what sowing looks like in general.

It is varied and unpredictable. It is daily grind and sweat coupled with moments of victory and seasons of kicking clumps of lifeless dirt. Sometimes in sowing, the seeds take root and grow and yield fruit. Other times they produce nothing. This is how it works.

Sow anyway.

Keep living in obedience to God. You may not see the sprouts of your efforts. You may not yet see the fruit. But sow.

How can you start today? What can you pray about? When can you take time to listen to God's call? Can you write that email? Send that text? Ring that doorbell? Can you have that conversation, take that risk?

Sow your fields.

Time will move forward. The season will change. And maybe with the newness brought by Chronological Change, you will see the fruit of your labors.

* * *

Fruititation

Originally posted on *Ten Blue Eyes* blog, October 1, 2017

I turned my back to the class of fifth graders in order to write their responses on the marker board. The chatter continued behind me.

I had placed the students from my midweek church class into groups and had asked each to read from Genesis in their Bibles to discover what God made during each of the six days of creation.

"I have Day Three! We know it!" one of the boys shouted.

"Go ahead. What did you find in Genesis chapter one?"

"On the third day, God made land and vegetation."

I nodded and wrote with the smelly dry-erase marker again:

DAY 3—LAND AND VEGETATION.

"That's right." I confirmed. "Now, can you tell me in your own words what vegetation is?"

"Oh sure! Vegetation is what vegetables grow on, and fruititation is what fruit grows on."

I should have turned my back again, because I laughed out loud—

right to his young, eager face. A technique surely not recommended in the teacher handbook.

"You're right about the vegetation, but fruititation is not a word. Fruit grows on vegetation as well." I said, bursting his bubble and maybe wounding his pride.

But, I've got to admit, I like the word.

Fruititation.

It's really growing on me.

Lately, I've been thinking about fruit. The kind of fruit that we bear in our lives, and how it's seasonal, just like the kind of fruit we pick, whether from trees or the produce department.

A short time ago, I walked through the hallway at church, on a Sunday morning, and was stopped by a friend. She told me she's in a small group Bible study, and they are currently using my book, *Brownie Crumbs and Other Life Morsels*, as their study guide. I was shocked and humbled.

Really?

She went on to tell me that they'd been having such great conversations within the group and were learning so much. I thanked her and walked away in a daze.

My mind wandered back to the hours I sat in my home office with tight shoulders and an exhausted brain. It took me three years to write that book! I literally spent days in front of a blinking cursor pouring my heart onto the page. I devoted time, tears, and cash preparing for the book launch.

One specific night, I stayed up well past midnight adjusting margins and headers, section by section, in my manuscript. It was tedious, boring, and frustrating work. I did not enjoy it. I remember being tired and annoyed.

I came back to the present and walked up the stairwell in the church that leads to and from the children's' classrooms. I had just dropped my own children off, and was now heading back up the steps. I passed two kids carrying their Bibles and curriculum. I wrote the curriculum they carried. The kids had their arms wrapped around it as they walked past me on the steps.

Again, my mind flashed back to the season before that curriculum was finished. I spent months writing the content, years teaching it and fine-tuning it, a solid year giving it a "makeover," and learning graphic design tricks and tools to make that possible. I put a lot of sweat equity into that curriculum.

Now, preteens, whom I don't even know, are carrying it with them to class on a Sunday morning and unknowingly passing the author on the steps on their way.

Could this be the culmination of fruititation?

Is this the wonderful cycle of bearing fruit?

Those tedious and seemingly wasteful hours of mundane and difficult work are important. In fact, they are more than important.

They are a *vital* part of the fruititation cycle.

Vital how? Vital because during those tedious tasks, the not-yet fruit was being tended. It wasn't time for the fruit to be picked, but time for it to be watered, cultivated, lovingly pruned, and painstakingly nurtured.

The fruit wasn't yet ripe. It was out of season. And being out of season usually means it can't be seen. It's not ready.

But that doesn't mean it isn't growing.

David, the psalmist, wrote about this in Psalm 1:1-3:

"Blessed is the one who does not walk in step with the wicked or stand in the way that sinners take or sit in the company of mockers, but whose delight is in the law of the Lord, and who meditates on his law day and night. That person is like a tree planted by streams of water, which yields its fruit in season and whose leaf does not wither—whatever they do prospers."

David mentions the tree that is planted and prosperous. But, he also mentions that the tree yields its fruit in season.

In season.

Not always. Sometimes the tree does not have visible hanging fruit. But it's still a fruit tree.

Sometimes my efforts are not publically visible either. They are margin-moving, cursor-crunching, photo-editing, head-gripping, tear-rendering, heart-stirring moments of cultivation.

Sometimes, the fruititation cycle in my life has nothing to do with writing, but with raising kids, cultivating my marriage, planting seeds of deep and meaningful friendships, and tending the soil of my own heart. It looks like difficult, honest conversations that would be easier to avoid, midnight touches of warm foreheads and beeps of the thermometer, tough love and deliberate discipline that wrings your heart into a knot, intentional time set aside for listening and truly seeing the needs of a friend, and daily surrender to selfish desires.

It's a struggle. A daily toil.

But the cultivation leads to the culmination of fruititation.

The fruit becomes visible. But only for a time. It won't last forever. It's just ripe for a bit.

But oh, how fun it is to see others enjoy it!

I am thankful for the moments when the fruit of my life is juicy, and ripe, and ready. But I'm also thankful for the reminder to press on in my daily, mundane, unnoticed, and often frustrating cultivating efforts.

Because they are vital.

Without them, fruititation is just a made-up word.

*   *   *

Chosen Change is probably the type of change I struggle with the least. Could that be because I've had more control over it? Yes, probably. We all like control, and if we feel like we're in control of the change, it feels less aggressive.

Examples of Chosen Change are: getting married, changing jobs, starting a family, taking on a commitment like a volunteer opportunity, working toward a dream or a goal, etc. They are usually positive events, unlike the Catastrophic Change examples.

My tools for dealing with Chosen Change are pretty simple. Believe and Receive.

Any type of change would benefit from employing these tools, but in Chosen Change, if we are insisting on remaining in control of our change, then it's a good practice to remind yourself it's not all about you in the first place. We can do that if we Believe and Receive.

We can Believe that the Chosen Change in our lives is what God desires for us. I hope that if I have chosen to make a change in my life, that I have first prayed about it and sought God's will in it. Actually prayed. Not said I was going to pray. Not thought about praying. But, actually prayed. I shouldn't move forward if I don't believe it's where or what God has for me. And I can Believe He will lead me into the Chosen Change that He desires for my life.

When I face a big decision, or a fork in the road where I must make a Chosen Change, I exercise a routine. I list the pros and cons, I talk to trusted friends and family and glean their opinions and thoughts. But most importantly, I pray. I ask God what He desires for my life. I ask Him to guide me and lead me. Then I make a decision (not immediately, but after I've done these things and given it some time). I don't tell anyone but

God my decision for awhile. I keep it between us. I talk to Him about it. I ask Him to confirm this choice in my heart with His perfect peace if that's what He would have me to do. Then I wait for a few days. I sleep on it. I continue living. I proceed as if the decision is made, only it has not been announced.

After a few days, I often will feel an overwhelming sense of peace and joy. God is confirming this decision in my life. Then I feel freedom to share the news with others.

Other times, restlessness descends on me. I churn inside, and realize this is not the best decision. I thank God for giving me clarity, and I ask Him to help me try again with another option.

This method of Believing is not something I present to you as "the way" to face Chosen Change. It's not in the Bible in so many words and therefore I'm not sharing it as truth. Yes, we are told in the Bible to pray and seek God, but this method is more something I've been taught by wise people, and have practiced over the years.

No matter your exact method for finding what you Believe to be God's will for you in a Chosen Change, what is most important, is that we truly Believe we are choosing what is honoring to Him.

*   *   *

Behold! I Stand at the Door and Ring the Doorbell
Originally posted on *Ten Blue Eyes* blog, on June 7, 2012

It's fun to mess with your kids.

Ever since we moved to a different house, our family has repeated a new trick that has yet to get old.

We now have two doorbells: one at the front door, and one in the garage by the house door. The chime sounds exactly the same no matter which doorbell you push, so of course we've been driving each other insane by ringing the garage doorbell and sending whichever gullible family member is closest to the front door. And nobody is there. It's hilarious!

This evening, I got our son with the trick once and then the second time he came looking for me in the garage. I tried to duck down behind the trashcan but I wasn't quick enough so I earned a "Mooooommmmm, I knew it was you!"

A bit later I had my husband ring the bell while I was with our son and it didn't fool him for a minute. He knew it was his dad. But, he's not able to completely outwit his parents yet. We sent our three-year-old out to garage (she can barely even reach the doorbell!) and while our son was changing into his baseball uniform near the front door (why he changes his clothes there, we don't know!) and when he was down to his undies, our daughter rang the doorbell with Mommy and Daddy both in plain view of our son. He looked from one of us to the other and his eyes got huge as he took off down the hall. Gotcha!!

Ahhh, fun times.

Here's the thing. I got to thinking about it while doing dishes one day (when I was not interrupted by a doorbell!) Sometimes in life we're looking for direction. As Christians, we say we're searching for "God's will." We have options, but we're not really sure if we're supposed to go toward "Door Number One," or "Door Number Two." We think we hear God's leading, but the chimes sound the same. How do we know what God's will is?

My dad has always told me that if you want to be in God's will, then you probably are. I like that. What he means is that if you're truly trying to honor God and live in obedience to Him, then you most likely are.

God's not going to trick us and ring a doorbell and run away. He's not going to send us to an empty front porch and make us feel idiotic. Instead, our Heavenly Father loves us and desires for us to live in righteousness and obedience. He will help guide us if we're truly seeking His direction.

But we still have to move when the doorbell rings.

We can't just sit back in our La-Z-Boy or continue with our housework while listening to the call of the bell. At some point we've got to move.

Romans 12:2 says:

"Do not conform to the pattern of this world, but be transformed by the renewing of your mind. Then you will be able to test and approve what God's will is—his good, pleasing and perfect will."

Test and approve. See, we have to try the doors. God's not going to drag us to the right door. We have to move. And we have to trust that He's not going to trick us. He loves us and will gently guide us as we honor Him with our actions.

Our Heavenly Father desires our obedience. He has a perfect will and if we want to walk in it, then we probably are. He won't deceive us with the call of the doorbell.

I wish I could say the same for my family!

*   *   *

The other tool for Chosen Change is Receive. We can first Believe that the change we are moving into is what God desires for us, and then we can Receive His help, comfort, love, grace, and peace through it.

God offers His presence to us at all times, free of charge. He delights in being with us! When we move into a season of Chosen Change, we should never forget to Receive God's blessings and love through it.

Even if it's a hard love, and things don't go as we wish. Even if the Chosen Change ends up being a bust, God won't fail you.

If you Believe a season of Chosen Change is what God has called you to, where He has led you, and what is in obedience to Him, then awesome. Now look for and Receive the fruits of that Belief.

One year for Christmas, my parents and Kraig and I gave Karly and Kenzie a gift certificate stating that Grandma and I would be taking them to Chicago over Christmas break to the American Girl store. We told the girls they could each pick out their own doll. They were ecstatic! The girls wrapped their little arms around my neck and squeezed me tight. Kenzie then looked into my eyes and sweetly said, "Mommy, can we buy the dollie that we pick out too?"

Oh, precious girl. Yes! Of course we're going to buy it too! We're not taking you to Chicago to dangle a gift in front of you and then leave the desired doll in the display case. We're bringing her home! She's going to be yours.

Kenzie Believed and then was thrilled to also Receive.

Receiving from God is also a wonderful gift. Once we Believe, we can enjoy what He offers to us. What might this look like?

It looks like letting God comfort and strengthen you as you walk into the boardroom at your new job. Like accepting peace as a blessing as you invest in a new relationship. Gaining wisdom as you attend the birthing class at the local hospital. Recognizing the new friend in your child's life as the one you've been asking God to send. Seeing a family member, whom you've been imparting hard love to for as long as you can remember, make a great decision because of your influence.

It's choosing to look for, and then accepting, the fruit of your faithfulness to God, and His faithfulness to you. His love, comfort, grace, hope, help, and peace. But it requires noticing. Receiving. Accepting.

God's fruit that He provides to those who choose to Receive is beautiful and bountiful. His gifts make my eyes twinkle and my heart race like those of my daughters as they stared at the display cases of dolls from which they could choose.

You Believed this was God's direction for your life. Now you can accept His gifts through it.

They're yours to keep for your very own.

Receive them with delight.

*   *   *

Slice of Hope: Catastrophic Change: Trust and Adjust, Chronological Change: See and Sow, Chosen Change: Believe and Receive eight

letting go
and
moving forward

I Don't Want to Let Go

Originally Posted on *Ten Blue Eyes* blog, June 13, 2013

Hi. My name is Christy and I struggle with letting go.

Hi, Christy.

I mean, I get excited about new things, but I don't like having to let go of what is familiar and comfortable and safe. Change can be scary, particularly if there are unknowns ahead. Like, if I can't picture what my routine will look like in the next stage, or what my purpose will be in a new season of life, I start to fret.

Please … tell us more.

I guess, well, I mean … I feel like I don't want to let go of what is certain because what if I don't like the next step as much as I like this one? How can I be sure it's safe to let go? But yet, as time marches on, I'm simply forced to let go of some things.

(Christy starts biting her nails.)

All right, I don't actually have a support group. But, I do have a husband, whom I asked one day why he thinks I feel sad during times of change, like on my kids' birthdays or last days of school. He said it's because I have issues. This made us both chuckle. Maybe I should get a support group. They'd probably be nicer.

But I don't think I'm the only one who feels this way. Women tend to agree with me. Please, someone tell me (or at least tell my husband) that I'm not alone.

We ladies can sometimes struggle with change ... and in particular, the changes that force us to let go. The act of letting go of a season of life, comfortable routine, or familiar territory challenges us. We'd prefer to keep a white-knuckled grip on our children, dreams, schedules, plans, hopes, and security. Trading the familiar for the unknown can be a bit unnerving.

This time of year always makes me feel sentimental too. Another school year has come to an end and I've seen kids that I used to babysit wear caps and gowns. Nostalgia strikes as my own son reaches a grade I can clearly remember being in myself (and not that long ago, either)! I am once again slapped with the reminder that time marches on more quickly than I'd like it to. I'm forced to let go of this stage and phase and usher in the new.

That kind of scares me.

But, wouldn't you know, I've found comfort and reassurance. Not from my husband or my imaginary support group, but from my Heavenly Father through a wonderful hymn reminding me of His truth.

As I stood with a group of ladies in a Bible study that I attend, we sang the hymn, "Praise to the Lord, the Almighty," and one of the lines struck a deep chord in me.

"Hast thou not seen how thy desires e'er have been

Granted in what He ordaineth"

I've thought about those lyrics countless times in the last few weeks. It's two short lines with a lot of meaning. In other words, it's saying:

"Hey! Haven't you noticed that God has provided peace and joy for you in every stage of your life, good *and* bad, up until this moment? He has basically made your desires fit with his will. What makes you think He won't be faithful to guide you and give you peace and joy in the next stage of life? Let go and move on, dummy!"

(You can see why my translation hasn't made it into the hymnal just yet.)

So, as I continue to replay that wonderful hymn and it's truth in my mind, I've found comfort and been reminded of God's faithfulness. It's hard to let go and to take steps into the unknown, but I trust that my God will go before me. He will lead me with His loving hand.

"Search me, God, and know my heart; test me and know my anxious thoughts. See if there is any offensive way in me, and lead me in the way everlasting." (Psalm 139:23-24)

So, let me ask you something, Christy.

(Imaginary Support Group leader leans back in her chair and crosses her legs. The rest of the imaginary group members lean in close to listen....)

Christy, hast thou not seen how thy desires e'er have been granted in what He ordaineth?!

Yes.

Yes, I have seen. With that in mind, may I look forward to the days ahead with joy and anticipation, as I trust in Him who leads me.

*   *   *

I never anticipated struggling to release the nursing of my babies. I didn't even think much about this before I had children, but once I did, and began to nurse them, I also began to dread its end. Maybe because weaning and allowing the milk to dry up signified the end of the infant stage. Or that providing that milk to sustain my children and help them grow gave me a sense of motherly pride. Nursing also brought bonding moments as that

201

child and I sat physically close, my arms wrapped around them. Regardless of the reason, I dreaded weaning my babies.

The strongest dread hit when the time came to wean my last baby. I wasn't positive, at that time, that she'd be my last, but I knew of the possibility. I had nursed her for fourteen months, and I hated the thought of being done.

But Kenzie, at barely over a year old, knew it was time and she taught me a lesson that day. One that I replay in moments when I'm dreading a new season. One that gently slapped me on the face, encouraging me to snap out of it, and move forward.

I sat in the La-Z-Boy, nursing Kenzie and knowing it was probably the last time. My sadness hung over me like a dark cloud. Tears threatened to trickle down my cheeks. But Kenzie squirmed and pushed away from me. She was a like a little ray of sunshine pushing out from behind the cloud. She twisted and wiggled and slid off of my lap and then ran, with her adorable "Frankenstein arms out in front" form to the pantry. She opened the door, and pulled out the food she really wanted. The thing she preferred over Mommy's milk.

Frosted Mini-Wheats.

I had followed her into the kitchen and now stood there and laughed. As she brought me the box of cereal and pointed to it making sure I understood her desire, I smiled. *This kid wants a bowl of Frosted Mini-Wheats. And she's able to eat them! Perhaps she is done with my milk. Perhaps it's time to move forward and let go!*

Now, when I'm not sure it's time for my kids to try a new thing, such as swimming without a life-jacket, or hanging out at a friend's birthday party whom I don't know well, or accept the responsibility of having a bank account, or phone plan, or allowance, I just think about those Frosted Mini-Wheats.

Moving forward and letting go is rough—like the hard, crunchy side of a Mini-Wheat biscuit. It's not the best part, but it's good. There's another side to it as well. And it's full of sweetness and delight!

*　　　*　　　*

In This Corner

Originally posted on *Ten Blue Eyes* blog, on November 13, 2012

I am going to be very honest here. Not that I usually lie. But, I like to write about something after I've got it neatly figured out in my mind. I prefer to organize my thoughts and feelings in a nicely gift-wrapped package and then deliver them onto my blog's doorstep for others to enjoy.

This post, however, is not yet in the gift box. I'm struggling to shove it into the "figured out" section of my cranium. I continue to mull over it and have concluded, at least for the time being, that I can't neatly package it. So I guess I'll just dump the contents of my brain out onto my blog and see what happens.

My conflict comes in the form of two little girls who create two very strong emotions in me. Those emotions exist on the complete opposite ends of the "feelings spectrum." I cannot understand how I can have both emotions dwell so strongly in my heart and mind when they are so polar opposite.

In one corner, I have frustration. My daughters, ages two and four, are always with me. I'm a stay-at-home mom and my daughters, are *always* with me. When I wake up, when I go to the restroom, when I take a shower, when I eat, when I exercise, when I drive ... you get the idea.

Sometimes I just would like to have a minute to myself when no little voice interrupts my conversation or my train of thought. In fact, my train of thought has been derailed so often that I'm not even sure it's on the tracks anymore. I'm getting tired of stoking the firebox and I feel as if my head may literally spew smoke. *I just want to be left alone.*

In the other corner ... *I don't want to be left alone!* I absolutely *love* being a mommy. It's my favorite stage of life so far and I'm living my dream. My husband is amazing and our son is enjoying second grade and I have the privilege of staying home with our two daughters. It's wonderful. I dread the day, in a few years, when my girls will both be in school and these precious preschool days will be done. The thought almost brings tears to my eyes.

How can this be?!

How can I feel both frustration and elation so strongly at the same time?

I don't know, but I'm telling you that they are both in the ring. They are duking it out every day. I want to hush my girls as they interrupt me for the 823rd time in a day and at the same time I want to scoop them up and snuggle them for hours. I want to be left alone so that I can do what I want to do for an evening, but when I am gone I find myself missing my children deeply and thinking about them often. When I see pictures of my kids as babies, I lament that their infant stages are behind us while at the same time wanting to dance with joy that their infant stages are behind us.

Seriously, my mommy emotions sometimes repel like two magnets with the same poles. They push at each other inside of me and cause me such confusion, joy, grief, happiness, and exhaustion.

I don't know yet how to neatly package these emotions. I can't reconcile them in my own mind let alone gift-wrap them to deliver neatly to others.

I guess that's motherhood. It's a confusing, conflicting, beautiful mess. And now that I've got my thoughts laying in a heap I realize that it's not so bad after all.

It's the gift that matters anyway, not the way it's wrapped.

*   *   *

When I'm struggling with letting go of a season of life, I call to mind the privilege that it was to experience that season in the first place. This sounds so "Suzy Sunshine" of me, but it helps.

I've always believed that gratitude is a game-changer in most any situation, and it's no exception in letting go. If we view the life and seasons we've been given as a privilege, not our right, then gratitude aids us in helping to let them go.

It's like playing that White Elephant or Dirty Bingo party game where you can steal other people's presents if you like them better than your own. You may have had a gift you liked in your possession for one minute. When Uncle Bill steals it from you, you feel the loss. Come on, Uncle Bill! But, you know, it was a gift in the first place! A privilege, and not your right.

Life is a gift to us. All of it. It's a privilege to be alive. It's not our right. It's not owed to us. It's a gift.

Gratitude for that gift can ease the pain of letting it go. Even if it's a party-sized loss.

*   *   *

Bear Cub on a Barbie Bike

Originally posted on *Ten Blue Eyes* blog, June 1, 2012

Down the street my little bear cub rode on the pretty, pink and purple Barbie bike with its matching girly training wheels. It should have been ever so cute.

Instead it was cringe-worthy.

The bear cub on the bike wasn't my little, pigtailed, three-year-old daughter, but instead her tall-for-his-age seven-year-old brother. His knees rose above the handlebars with every turn of the pedals. The training wheels gradually bent upward as his body weight tipped from one side to the other. His red helmet clashed with the pink and purple paint. Frankly, he looked pretty ridiculous.

My bear cub on a Barbie bike.

I call him my bear cub because I turned into a Mother Bear that afternoon. If I'm being honest with myself, I've been a protective and fiercely loving Mother Bear for seven years.

That's really the whole problem here.

During Karson's leukemia and chemotherapy, we hibernated. I was a Mother Bear with a sick little cub and I did all that I could to keep him safe and sound while he healed. Our hibernation excluded bike rides because they could lead to falls and scrapes and bruises, dangerous for a child who often had low platelets and was very fragile. Since he never asked to ride a bike, we simply didn't put him on one.

Today, he's a healthy and strong young man who was the tallest child in his first grade class. He plays basketball and baseball and swims like a fish. He's big for his age, and you'd never know by looking at him that he fought cancer as a preschooler. He's growing up right before our eyes.

But he still can't ride a bike.

And one thing he learned in first grade was that his friends can.

Now he knows what he's missing and he wants to learn, desperately enough that he was willing to ride his little sister's girly bike. We'd tried his own bigger and boyish bike over and over again to no avail. He just didn't have the experience of riding a smaller bike to know what it felt like to balance without training wheels. My husband even tried putting training wheels on his bike, but bikes built for eighty-two-pound kids just aren't made for training wheels.

So there we were on a sunny Sunday afternoon going down the sidewalk in our neighborhood. My son on the bike and me walking behind with my eyebrows raised and jaw clenched, just waiting for the poor training wheels to finally burst off and the exhausted bike, with its rider, to collapse to the ground.

In fact, he did very well. Granted, he had to get off the bike every once in a while to kick the bent training wheels back down so they'd reach the ground, but otherwise, it was smooth sailing.

Until he rode by a yard full of kids.

Now, thankfully, my little bear cub obliviously pedaled past the conversation that took place amongst his peers. But I heard. I was walking far enough behind that by the time I reached the kids, I could hear their laughter, see their pointing, and understand their mocking comments about the big boy riding a small pink bike. Oh, did my Mother Bear instincts kick in! I kept walking and kept my mouth shut, but I sure wanted to go grizzly on those little kids!

I held on to my tongue that day, and other days my husband and I held on to the back of my son's bike, desperately trying to help him learn to balance.

But it's hard to know when to let go.

I probably should have let go years ago and allowed my little cub to ride a bike, even though it was scary for his mother. I probably am not a good one to help him learn to ride his big bike now because I'm afraid to let go and watch him fall.

But I can't hold on forever. It wouldn't be healthy if I did.

In fact, I've had to let go more often. I've had to let go of his bike seat, and I've had to let go, albeit ever so gradually, of my children. It's good for them to learn to ride bikes, even when they fall and get hurt. It's good for them to grow up and become more independent and confident, even when it hurts my heart.

It's hard to know when to hold on and when to let go.

But letting go is necessary. I'm going to have to send my children off to scary places, like second grade, and heaven forbid, middle school and high school. It's why I get choked up at the end of *Toy Story 3* when Andy's toys all wave goodbye to him as he heads off to college. I'm just afraid I'm not going to handle my own kids growing up with the grace and poise of Buzz Lightyear.

But, grow up they will. I really wouldn't want it any other way. I know those who have children whom they have watched graduate from high school, enter the work force, and walk down the aisle will laugh at me and think I ain't seen nothing yet.

Please, don't remind me. I must take this one day at a time. One letting go at a time.

I've stopped hibernating now, and I'm doing better at allowing my little bear cubs to roam on their own and grow to be more independent and confident.

Whether Barbie bikes, high school graduations, or wedding days, I pray that this Mother Bear will enjoy *both* the holding on and the letting go as my bear cubs grow up before my eyes.

*   *   *

As you may have surmised by now, letting go is a continual struggle in my life. Especially the type of letting go that requires moving into a new season of life—when the change means forever leaving a season behind.

I've already talked about this some in the Change chapter of this book when I share about Chronological Change. If you remember, the tools for dealing with Chronological Change are See and Sow—to truly see the present, and to live in it before it's gone, and to sow in your mind and in your fields.

But the very last step of moving into a new season is to let go of the old season. This doesn't mean we don't remember the old season, or grieve it, or miss it. No, if you're a human being, then you have a mind capable of memories and feeling emotions. That's how you were made! It's okay to remember and to feel. In fact, it's a great thing! But we also have to move into the new season by *living* in that season. We can be both physically and mentally present in the new season while still remembering the old. It's all part of the process of letting go.

There's a difference between moving on, and moving forward. Not to brag or anything, but I'm in the company of Albert Einstein with this thought (this sentence may be the only time I'm mentioned with Einstein. Savor it.)

He said, "It is the same with people as it is with riding a bike. Only when moving can one comfortably maintain one's balance."

Moving forward indicates you've already been somewhere, and by moving, you're continuing the journey. It doesn't mean the past is forgotten, but that you're now moving forward from it.

Moving on sounds a bit more like you're leaving the past behind.

You've finished the delivery, you've made the stop, you've completed the task. Now you move on and forget. This is fine if you're a pizza delivery person, but as a general rule, we can't just expect to move on to the next stop in life and forget everything else.

We cannot deny that the past happened. We should not deny the good or the bad. The past, the stages and seasons we loved and lived, are always going to be a part of us! The stages and seasons we loathed are too. That's okay. We shouldn't move on from them, but move forward in spite of them, through them, with them.

I often call to mind 1 Corinthians 4:16-18 in times of change and letting go. It reads,

> Therefore we do not lose heart. Though outwardly we are wasting away, yet inwardly we are being renewed day by day. For our light and momentary troubles are achieving for us an eternal glory that far outweighs them all. So we fix our eyes not on what is seen, but on what is unseen, since what is seen is temporary, but what is unseen is eternal.

Yes, this passage is about dealing with hardships, but also about change and letting go. You see, as we live, we are "wasting away." Each day we are moving closer to the end of this earthly life. But inwardly, those of us who are in Christ are being "renewed day by day."

This renewal is a process. It's preparing us for eternity and shaping us to be more like Christ on this Earth. We can't always detect the process or see the change, but it's happening. Our bicycle wheels are barely spinning, but it's enough to keep us upright.

Being renewed each day by Jesus requires letting go of what we were yesterday. Not denying it happened, but moving forward anyway.

A sweet little girl, a friend of our daughters, was learning to water ski last summer. I sat in the boat with my girls and our friends, who were driving and shouting out instructions to the little girl. My husband was in the water trying to help her get her skis on and learn how to hold the rope.

And she did it! She got up on the skis and took a long ride around the lake. In fact, a very long ride. I realized we had not clearly explained that she only needed to let go of the rope when she'd finished. Simply let go. But we didn't make this clear to her, and so, she never did. She skied on and on. After awhile, her little body bent forward at the hips and she looked exhausted.

"You can let go!" her aunt yelled from the boat.

"Do you want to let go of the rope?" my girls yelled as they made a motion with their own hands of dropping the handle.

She wasn't understanding, and so she skied on, looking as if she were about to break in half.

Her uncle, the boat driver, wasn't sure if he should stop the boat because we weren't positive if she wanted to be done, and getting up again would be hard work. So she just kept on going.

Finally, we looped back around to our shoreline and stopped. She fell slowly into the water, still not letting go of the rope until she was forced to by the plunge.

"My back hurts! I'm so tired!" she said.

We all laughed. She could have stopped long ago if she would have just let go of the rope.

I get it, girl!

Sometimes I want to move forward into a new season, and I know it will be exciting once I get there, but I just don't want to let go of the rope. I'm comfortable where I am. I'm not sure how the transition will feel. I like the way things are going now. Even if my back hurts and I'm tired of the fight, I'd rather hold on and be safe then let go into the unknown.

It's not just about the unknown. Sometimes it's about the sadness I feel that a particular stage is ending. I've loved it so much, whether it be having preschoolers at home, or working outside the home, or watching my children compete in a sport that they have now finished, that I don't want to face the sadness by letting go of the rope.

But facing the sadness offers the chance for joy in remembering, and anticipation of what's ahead. Just as looking grief in the eyes helps bring healing, admitting the sadness of leaving a season of life helps us to move forward with it. When we face the sadness, we also acknowledge the goodness of that particular season, and then hopefully that turns into gratitude that it happened!

As Dr. Seuss says, "Don't cry because it's over, smile because it happened."

I say, if you want to cry too, that's okay. Cry, laugh, remember, grieve, and then move forward. And if you need to cry, laugh, remember, grieve, and move forward again later this afternoon, that's okay. This isn't a one-time deal. You may have to let go of the rope multiple times. You may not realize you've grabbed hold of it once again.

Letting go is a process. It's a healthy and natural process at that.

As I said in the Chronological Change chapter, Genesis 1 shows us that God created the seasons and time on the fourth day of creation. (Genesis 1:14) They were part of the original creation, before the fall, when sin entered the world. A part of the original design. So, this tells me that even if sin and death never entered this world, seasons and time still would have existed. Now, they would have been different in the sense that they would not have led to death, as time does for us now, but they would have still been part of creation. Seasons still would have been a beautiful framework by which to live, and this encourages me.

We see cycles in life when one season begins, and another one ends. When the leaves fall off the trees, they yield to winter. When the snow melts and the flowers bloom, winter yields to spring. And so forth. If we're still holding on and trying to live in the fall, we're going to miss every other season.

Letting go is part of living.

I always remind myself that the alternative to letting go and moving forward is holding on and stagnating. Stagnant is never a positive word, is it? Nobody desires to drink from a stagnant pond that is holding on to its growths. Instead, we want to drink from a babbling stream that is moving, and fresh, and purified. Jesus didn't call Himself "Stagnant Water," but "Living Water." (John 7:38) Stagnating and holding on to the past doesn't seem appealing anymore, does it?

So how do we let go of the rope?

We process the journey, remember the moments, grieve the loss, move forward. Process, remember, grieve, move forward.

Opening our grip and releasing the rope frees our hands to grab the present in front of us.

When we're free to move forward and live in the present, we're ready to open the front door and usher in Life, with all of its Opportunities.

We shouldn't put it off any longer.

With this life, it's rarely a piece of cake, but I know we can whip up something from the pantry.

I'd better preheat the oven.

*　　　*　　　*

Slice of Hope: Letting go of the past, while still acknowledging and remembering it, frees our hands to grasp the present. Then we are free to move forward, without striving to move on.

Cakewalk

applying the talk to your walk

discussion/application questions

Chapter 1

Worry and Anxiety

- Do you struggle with worry? What triggers or thoughts cause you to worry most often?

- Do you find yourself "waiting for the other shoe to drop," and living in anxiety? What circumstances magnify this for you?

- Are you a funnel worrier or a fountain worrier?

- What is one thing you are worried about right now? What do you know to be true in that situation? Are you incorporating that truth into your worry? What Bible verses help you in times of worry?

- The Slice of Hope for this chapter is, "When we share our worries with a trusted friend, and replace our anxiety with what we know to be true, we can begin to live in the peace which Jesus daily provides." Name at least one trusted friend with whom you can share your worries. Have you done so lately? If not, why not?

Chapter 2

Guilt and Regret

- Name one situation in which you have felt guilt within the past month. What did that guilt stem from?
- Are there any situations or relationships in your life where you should ask for forgiveness or restoration?
- "Truth is a good fighter to send into battle when Guilt begins to rear her ugly head." Where do you need to employ truth in a situation where you feel guilt? What is that truth?
- The Slice of Hope for this chapter is, "Grace and forgiveness can defeat guilt and regret. We need to accept them into our struggle, and then allow them to succeed." Have you accepted grace in the situations in which you have failed? If not, what is holding you back? If so, have you allowed grace to defeat the guilt?

Chapter 3

Discontentment and Insecurity

- Are you currently struggling with discontentment in this season of your life? If not, that's great! What do you feel is your purpose and how has that helped you with contentment? If so, have you shared your thoughts and feelings with a trusted friend? Have you shared them with God?

- What is an area or circumstance in your own life that didn't turn out the way you expected or dreamed? Have you grieved that loss? If not, give yourself permission to do so.

- Do you believe God can use your ordinary for His extraordinary? If not, what is causing your disbelief?

- What is one "good" you've compared with someone else's "good" this week? What is one "bad" you've compared with someone else's "bad" this week?

- The Slice of Hope for this chapter is, "God sees you and loves you right where you are. Don't compare yourself to others! Stay in your lane while validating the successes and struggles of others. Loving God is obeying Him, even if the tasks seem lesser than another's, or too ordinary to matter. Obedience to God is extraordinary, after all." Are you obeying God today?

Chapter 4

Love and Like

- Words can hurt or help. What is one way you've used your words to help someone this week? What is one way you've used your words to hurt someone this week?

- We can become easily offended if we don't take the time to truly listen to and consider the other person's point of view. Have you been offended by someone recently? Have you taken time to really consider their motives or true meaning?

- Name one relationship in your life where you could employ mercy. What are you waiting for?

- The Slice of Hope for this chapter is, "Healthy relationships require effort. From the toil of giving mercy, showing grace, offering forgiveness, and listening humbly, we can reap a harvest of sweet laughter and joy." Are you currently giving mercy, showing grace, and offering forgiveness to those you are closest to? How could you improve?

- Are you a humble listener? Who is a good listener in your life? What do you think makes them a good listener? How can you take practical steps to be a better listener?

- Name at least one relationship where you are experiencing laughter and joy on a regular basis. If you can't name one, why do you think this is?

Chapter 5

Loss and Anger

- What personal losses would you say have had the greatest impact on your life?

- Have you ever experienced a loss that caused you to become angry? With whom were you angry?

- Have you ever been angry with God? If so, how did you cope? Did you talk to God about your anger?

- The Slice of Hope in this chapter is: "Sometimes we pray and live through gritted teeth. Continue anyway." Why do you think it's important to continue to live and move forward despite loss and anger?

- How has gratitude helped you to diffuse anger in your own life? If it has not, what is one practical step you can take to practice gratitude this week?

Chapter 6

Lamenting and Living

- What do you think the angel meant when he said, "Why do you look for the living among the dead?" in Luke 24:5? Remember, this is the passage where, after Christ's death and burial, the women go to Jesus' tomb.

- Have you ever felt as if you deserved something from God? What was it, and why did you feel that way?

- Knowing that we can never earn or deserve anything from God, what can you choose to let go of in the way of anger or bitterness?

- Have you accepted God's grace, which is completely free, and surrendered your life to Him? If not, why not?

- What are you lamenting now? Are you sharing your honest emotions with God and your loved ones? Remember, healthy lamenting can lead to redemption.

- The Slice of Hope for this chapter is, "Don't look for the living among the dead. Lament and live while remembering the eternal hope Christ brings through redemption. Don't strive for God's peace and love; accept them daily." How can you apply this to your life this week?

- What does it mean to have an eternal hope? How can this hope help you today?

Chapter 7

Change and New Seasons

- The Slice of Hope for this chapter is, "Catastrophic Change: Trust and Adjust, Chronological Change: See and Sow, Chosen Change: Believe and Receive." Do you struggle with change, or enjoy and look forward to it?

- What Catastrophic Changes have you faced in your life? Which is most recent or painful?

- How can you apply the tools of "Trust" and "Adjust" to your Catastrophic Change? Do you truly trust that God is in control? If not, why not? Where do you need to adjust your perspective and then move forward?

- What Chronological Changes have been difficult for you?

- How can you use the tools of "See and Sow" in the Chronological Change that you are facing? Do you intentionally see what is in front of your face? If not, what is hindering you? Do you sow the reminders in your mind of an eternal perspective and that God gave us seasons for our benefit? Are you sowing in your fields? If so, how? If not, where can you begin to work? What dreams can you act upon?

- What Chosen Changes have affected your life recently?

- How can you use the tools of "Believe and Receive" in your Chosen Change? Do you believe God has led you into this Chosen Change? Have you received His peace and guidance in this Chosen Change? How specifically are you progressing to Receive?

Chapter 8

Letting Go and Moving Forward

- Do you struggle with letting go of a season and moving into the next, or are you usually more excited and ready for the change?

- When have you struggled to move into a new season? Are you currently facing such a struggle?

- Do you view your time as a right or as a privilege? How can you change this thinking to be more focused on gratitude for the privilege and blessings you've been given?

- How would you describe the difference between moving forward, and moving on?

- The Slice of Hope for this chapter is, "Letting go of the past, while still acknowledging and remembering it, frees our hands to grasp the present. Then we are free to move forward, without striving to move on." Is there anything in your past, or even in your present, that you are refusing to let go of? How can you begin the healthy process of letting go and moving forward today?

slices of hope

1. <u>Worry and Anxiety</u> - When we share our worries with a trusted friend, and replace our anxiety with what we know to be true, we can begin to live in the peace which Jesus daily provides.

2. <u>Guilt and Regret</u> - Grace and forgiveness can defeat guilt and regret. We need to accept them into our struggle, and then allow them to succeed.

3. <u>Discontentment and Insecurity</u> - God sees you and loves you right where you are. Don't compare yourself to others! Stay in your lane while validating the successes and struggles of others. Loving God is obeying Him, even if the tasks seem lesser than another's, or too ordinary to matter. Obedience to God is extraordinary, after all.

4. <u>Love and Like</u> - Healthy relationships require effort. From the toil of giving mercy, showing grace, offering forgiveness, and listening humbly, we can reap a harvest of sweet laughter and joy.

5. <u>Loss and Anger</u> - Sometimes we pray and live through gritted teeth. Continue anyway.

6. <u>Lamenting and Living</u> - Don't look for the living among the dead. Lament and live while remembering the eternal hope Christ brings through redemption. Don't strive for God's peace and love; accept them daily.

7. <u>Change and New Seasons</u> - Catastrophic Change: Trust and Adjust. Chronological Change: See and Sow. Chosen Change: Believe and Receive.

8. <u>Letting Go and Moving Forward</u> - Letting go of the past, while still acknowledging and remembering it, frees our hands to grasp the present. Then we are free to move forward, without striving to move on.

acknowledgements

The process of writing and releasing a book is tedious. So many details and to-do lists sometimes make my head spin. But, I like the challenge, and I push toward the finish line with enthusiasm and energy. I go into "get 'er done" mode and work with dedication and swiftness. But, the one task that has proven to cause this non-procrastinator to slow down and procrastinate is writing the acknowledgements. Why? Because they are so important and heartfelt that I save them until the last possible moment. I don't want to forget anyone, or gloss over my gratitude too quickly. And so, as I offer these "thank you's," know that is it difficult to truly convey my deep sense of gratitude and appreciation for each.

To Matt Jacoby, Kenn Kington, Bekah Shaffer, Heather Gonzales, Mitch Kruse, Mark and Angela Vincenti, and Graham Daniels, thank you all for your kind endorsements of this book. I can't express how much your support means to me. I am humbled and honored by your words.

To Heather Bienz at Reagan 25 photography. Thank you for the headshots of this girl who would rather be behind the camera than in front of it! You do great work! Keep it up!

To my Book Launch Team and my Writing Group, your support and help means the world to me! Thanks for being, "my people."

To Krysta Young, thank you for graciously allowing us to invade your bakery, Sassie Cakes, and set up lights, a microphone, camera, and more to film my book trailer. You were so kind to us and you are an amazing cake creator. And, that peanut butter chocolate cookie dough, wow!

To Jaci Miller, your skillful edits of my manuscript made this book much stronger. You have a great eye for the technical aspects of writing, and yet you also have wisdom in helping me sharpen the message. I am thankful you are part of my team, and even more thankful you are my friend!

To Susan Rekeweg, your cover design has once again blown me away. You do such beautiful work! I've learned people really do judge a book by its cover, so I'm glad you're the one designing mine!

To Pappy, thank you for once again being my favorite (and dare I say oldest, at the age of 90!) proofreader. You are amazing and I love you!

To my favorite videographer and stylist team, my kids, Karson and Karly, who helped me film and edit my book trailer. Thank you! It was truly so much fun to work together (and sample cupcakes!). You are both smart, capable, and helpful kids. You make your mom proud in more ways than I can express. And though you didn't help with the book trailer, the same goes for you, Kenzie! You all three are a delight to me! At the printing of this book, you are ages 14, 10, and 9 (Kenzie, this book was released on your birthday!). I love how you each support me as I write, and how you are excited to share about my books with your friends and teachers. Thank you. Mommy loves you!

To the man who not only allowed me to share personal stories about him all throughout these pages, but also wrote the foreword (such a nice one!) and shares his very life with me. Kraig Cabe, you are my favorite! No relationship, other than the one I have with Jesus, has blessed me more than yours. You are so wise, funny, stable, and special. I'm so thankful for you, and how we've grown closer to the Lord and to each other since sharing those bites of wedding cake at our reception (I had to work cake in there somehow!). When you finally write your book that you've been "threatening me" with and share all the stories about me from your perspective, I'll write your foreword. Until then, I'm looking forward to living out our story together.

To the one who knows me best, my Heavenly Father, who has brought me hope and peace throughout the difficulties of this life, as well as joy and grace indescribable. Who confirms for me that it was good to have certain desires in my heart, and even better to choose to love and obey Him, I say thank you. God, this book is dedicated most of all to Your glory and honor.

ABOUT THE AUTHOR

Christy Cabe writes about life through an honest, observant, and down-to-earth voice. She has been known to make her readers cry and laugh within the span of a few moments as she focuses on truth, hope, and humor. Christy enjoys telling a good story in hopes that the reader will walk away encouraged and inspired to grow in their love for God, and for others. Her first book, *Brownie Crumbs and Other Life Morsels*, was released April 2017. The book spent a couple of days trending on the Amazon "Hot New Release" charts in the Christian Spiritual Growth category, even temporarily passing books by Francis Chan, Rick Warren, and Tim Tebow. Christy has a degree in educational ministries from Huntington University, drinks coffee every morning, and lives in Indiana with her husband, Kraig, and their three children.

You can find Christy's blog, *Ten Blue Eyes*, at christycabe.com

65369281R00144

Made in the USA
Middletown, DE
04 September 2019